Walking the Fine

Map

7 KEYS TO AN EXTRAORDINARY
LIFE

Your life is a masterpiece.
For the living,
Tonya Spence

By Tonya Spence

www.tonyaspencespeaks.com

ISBN: 978-0-9841121-9-7 1

Published by

Personality
INSIGHTS
PRESS

Book cover created by: Panagiotis Lampridis
Book cover photo by: Patty Stroming Recca
Dedication Photo by: APHA/Paint Horse Journal
Special thank you to Martha McGeehon for making the vision
of my cover a reality.

Editor: R.W. Jensen
solfire@phoenix-farm.com

PRINTED IN THE UNITED STATES OF AMERICA

Dedications

To my sweet Gentle Giant, thank you Dad for your unshakable love; it has changed me. I've spent a lifetime safely crawling into my Heavenly Father's arms knowing He was just like you. Because of you, the multitudes have encountered Him.

To my beautiful velvet brick, thank you Mom for always believing in your girl and modeling unspeakable faith, wisdom and courage. You've truly been our "Jesus wrapped in skin" and my best friend for life. I want to be just like you when I finally grow up!

To Tammy, Dondi and David, I can't imagine this life without you; you color my world beautiful! Your loyalty, selfless love and passion for family is a thread that runs deep in our blood . . . you've kept the legacy alive. I love you with all my heart.

To my sweetheart Tom, because of you I've known love. You've been the wind beneath my wings from "hello", turning my dreams into reality. As a man among all men, you've set an unreachable bar . . . *my heart is forever yours.*

Table of Contents

INTRODUCTION

I t was the Christmas season and within weeks, they chopped off my hair, changed my wardrobe, embezzled my beauty sleep, wrecked my social life and relocated me across the country. Yes, one morning I woke up and decided to be a flight attendant . . . but wondered if I'd joined the U.S. Marines! We were the new recruits chosen for a special training to be squeezed in by the end of the year. It was intense and crammed into half the time of their standard training. Between the lengthy classes, written tests, hours in simulated airplanes, administrative tasks and image overhauls, we were stretched thin and exhausted; many didn't make it. My attitude earned me the nickname 'Maverick.' I had the tenacity and determination of a defiant bulldog yet tried to sustain some sweet southern charm. Internally, I knew this wasn't the right career path for me but I silenced that voice. I wasn't following the desires of my heart but chasing a whim in my head that looked appealing to others. My peace was gone but I couldn't turn back now . . . everyone was watching and cheering me on.

The girls and I were given a week to pack, move, find a place to live and locate the three airports at our base . . . all before our first assignment. It was like watching The Three Stooges on steroids! It was crazy CHAOS! Dad lovingly dropped everything to help us with the long drive and move. His three day trip turned into a nine day nightmare; but he smiled every mile of the way. Little did he know how much his presence comforted my

Introduction

restless soul. The comedy began when our four car caravan pulled into a hotel in Nashville for the night.

I questioned Dad, "Why are we stopping in Nashville, that's not even near the direction we're headed?" Obviously, he had done all the driving while I did most the sleeping. He explained it was our half-way point to Washington. I was so confused. Then we figured it out. I thought I was moving to Seattle in Washington State, not Washington D.C.! We laughed till our tummy's hurt; and that story has gone down in family history.

It would be a far cry to say that was the last time I traveled down the

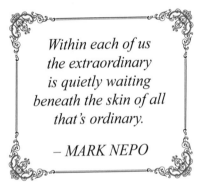

Within each of us the extraordinary is quietly waiting beneath the skin of all that's ordinary.

– MARK NEPO

wrong path. It wasn't the last time I chose an unsuitable profession or thought a 'good decision' would take me one place only to end up somewhere else. But somebody shout HALLELUJAH . . . I have jumped off that train! Today, my greatest passion is helping you take the leap into your abundant purpose with full assurance that you are ENOUGH.

When we march to the beat of someone else's drum and don't dance to the rhythm of our own song, the consequences are subtle yet very real. Dissatisfaction and complacency become our acceptable reality with grey skies leading to a place called No-Where. On one hand, it may pay the bills and help you accumulate material things, keep you busy and build surface relationships. It may even make you feel important, needed and accomplished. But my question to you is, "Does your heart sing?"

Every person is designed for a great purpose but few discover it. It's time for what we know to be true in our hearts to show up in our lives. Just going through the motions was never God's design for us. We must awaken a part of us we never knew was sleeping. Just like my earthly daddy had the right map to get me to my desired destination (Washington D.C.) safe and sound, your heavenly Father is ready to whisk you away to your promised land. He's prepared first class travel arrangements and is inviting you to partner with Him, not because of how "good" we have been but because how much He loves. He loves you more in a moment than anyone could in a lifetime and His dreams for you have no expiration date.

Our lives are to be masterpieces that transcend anything that is normal. Take, for example, a dancer in all their beauty and strength. They are able to leap and leave the ground for a moment in time. And even though they return back to the ground, they are not confined to it because they have taken flight into their personal purpose. As God's children we are called to take flight; to soar in our passions and purpose. We are to display to the world how great God is by giving life to the dreams He has birthed inside of us.

Now it's your turn. It's time to start living the extraordinary life created just for YOU! I love this definition for extraordinary which is:

> very unusual: very different from what is normal or
> ordinary. Extremely good or impressive. So
> unusual as to be remarkable.1

Introduction

When I look back on my life I want it to be anything but ordinary. Remarkable suits me just fine. Poet Mark Nepo wrote, "Within each of us the extraordinary is quietly waiting beneath the skin of all that's ordinary." Yes, like me, you may feel like you're getting a late start but what you begin doing today can completely alter all your tomorrows.

This book was written as a guide to help you unlock all the gifts and blessings inside of you. To lead you to a place you've never been but that has been waiting for your arrival.

By applying these simple yet timeless principles, you'll be empowered to live a life of ultimate fulfillment and significance. Become the Christopher Columbus of YOUR future and dare to lose sight of the shore. God is calling us to fall in love with the unknown, to walk off our map and land onto His . . .

. . . it's a place called Destiny.

http://www.thefreedictionary.com/extraordinary

FOREWORD

Every so often you meet an individual who is really special. I mean really special. They are not better than anyone else - because life is not a contest. But they are still special. There is just a kindness to some people that attracts others to themselves. I have known both men and women who have had an inner strength and beauty about them that goes beyond looks and words. It is deeper than that! You might say it is the "spirit" of that person which transcends the natural world that we can see and touch. Tonya Spence is that kind of person. She is the real deal! She is special!

Years ago when I worked with Zig Ziglar, I watched people be attracted to him. Zig has that kind of spirit. People wanted to shake his hand or have a picture with him. I genuinely believe they were hoping he would somehow magically "rub off" on them in some manner. And that is alright! He demonstrated life and energy and kindness and love toward everyone he met. People are attracted to that kind of person. That is the kind of person anyone would want to be around. You know...special!

Someone once wisely noted that when others see you coming they either say, "Oh boy", or "Oh no!" That is what I am talking about – having an aroma about you that attracts people to you because of the influence and difference you will make in their life!

Tonya has written a beautiful book which is a direct reflection of the kind of person she truly is! When you read this work, expect to be touched not only in your mind – but in your spirit as well. That is the kind of person Tonya is and that is the kind of influence this book will have in your life and will help you to become! You know...*special!*

Robert A. Rohm, Ph.D., *President*
Personality Insights, Inc.
Atlanta, GA

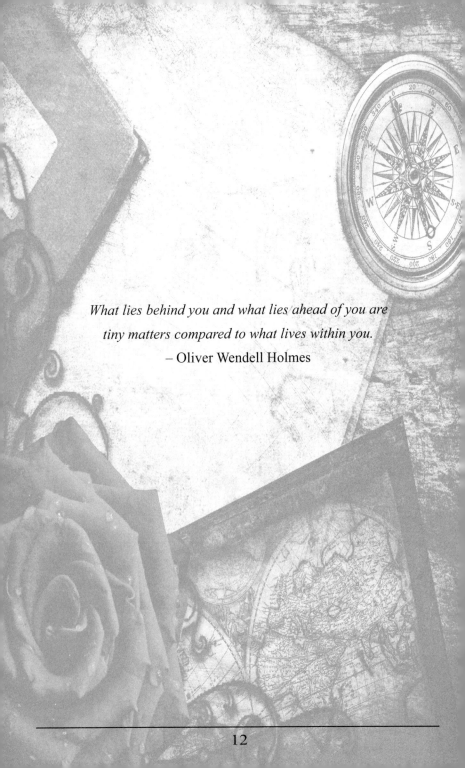

What lies behind you and what lies ahead of you are
tiny matters compared to what lives within you.
– Oliver Wendell Holmes

Key 1

Anchored In True Identity

Anchored In True Identity

Waking up to the aroma of Dad's homemade buttermilk pancakes and breakfast sausage smothered in hot syrup, alongside Saturday morning cartoons and superheroes, was a cherished tradition in our home. Batman and Robin, Wonder Woman and the Lone Ranger were enough to ignite the imagination of any youngster; something inside me resonated with them all. Even today, I still love getting whisked away by any superhero, pretending to be their chosen sidekick to help save the world. By trade, they're seemingly ordinary people that play typical roles in society. But that's only a facade; a cover-up for their real identity as humans with superpowers and abilities.

In the movie Man of Steel, Clark Kent (Superman) as a young 13 year old says to his earthly father, "Can't I just keep pretending I'm your son?" His father replies, "You are my son. But somewhere out there you have another father too, who gave you another name. And he sent you here for a reason, Clark. And even if it takes the rest of your life, you owe it to yourself to find out what that reason is." His father goes on to say, "Maybe there is more at stake here than our lives or the lives of others. When the world finds out what you can do it's gonna change everything; our beliefs,

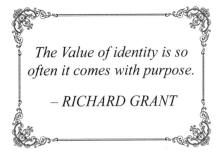

The Value of identity is so often it comes with purpose.

– RICHARD GRANT

our notions and what it means to be human . . . everything."

If I had to choose only one key to share with people of all ages, it would be this one, "Get anchored in your true identity." Knowing who you truly are at your core is monumental and second to nothing. To say applying this principle has changed my life would be an understatement. It continues to transform me on a daily basis. Walking in your true identity is the greatest journey of a lifetime and it never ends. When we recognize our lives exist from the inside/out and embrace who we are at a heart level, the tides turn in every area of our existence. When the big red S inscribed into the center of our being is unveiled, nothing is impossible.

ANCHORS AWAY MATE

Consider the anchor of a ship. No matter how magnificent and powerful a ship is on the outside, it's destined for destruction against the rocks in a stormy sea. However, it will endure the crashing waves if there's an anchor holding it firm, far beneath the surface, to the solid ground below. Being anchored in your God-given identity and self-worth are crucial to living an empowered life. No amount of money can buy it, knowledge can't unlock it, prestige can't access it and no one can attain it for you. It is a gift that can only be received by you. You are the only one that holds the proper key.

Proverbs 23:7 says it this way, "As a man thinks in his heart, so is he." In other words, you become what you behold. Your outer world is completely guided, dominated and showcased by your inner world. The thoughts you have and how you see yourself touches everything around you. The hundreds of choices you make on a daily basis, from the friends you choose, the words you speak, the clothes you wear, the career you pursue, the books you read, to the person you marry, are all results of your identity and self-worth.

There are areas in my life where I feel completely confident and assured while other areas seem to be a continual work in progress for me. Have you ever had a situation in your life persist longer than necessary because you just didn't want to deal with it head on? We may try to change jobs, attend another church, move to a new city or find 'better' friends but take my word for it; it just doesn't work . . . I've tried all the above. Like the lyrics from Clint Black's country song, "Wherever you go, there you are. You can run from yourself but you won't get far." The same issues will keep resurfacing because they've become rooted in our inner landscape that needs restoration. Once we surrender all that we are to Jesus, holding nothing back, the scenery begins to transform into something beautiful and whole. William Booth said it well, "The greatness of a man's power is the measure of his surrender."

STEP INTO HIS PHONE BOOTH

It reminds me of Clark Kent entering a phone booth and exiting as Superman. When we step into 'God's phone booth,' we experience an internal transformation that is far superior to anything produced through willpower or hard work. You see, only His perfect and powerful love can deal with our deepest fears and restore our God-given dignity and worth.

Until we personally discover the unconditional acceptance and approval of the Father, not based on behavior but on the finished work of Jesus, can we become empowered to reach our fullest potential.

The way we enter into our authentic identity is by living from the inside/out, that is, seeing yourself as God sees you RIGHT NOW! He already sees you as more than a conqueror, an overcomer, the salt and light of the world. You are a child of The King and the Most High God with full access to your inheritance. A new found confidence and courage are revealed as His bright red cape encompasses your heart. Through Jesus, you are now connected to 'The Source' for unlimited power and resources to live and write the story of your choice. This is the game changer for your future because when you know who you are, you know what you can do. Simply put, people do what they think!

Your outer world is entirely guided, dominated and showcased by your inner world.

The Bible says that God is able to carry out His purpose and do superabundantly more than all we dare ask or think; infinitely beyond our greatest prayers, hopes or dreams, by His power that is at work within us. It says God's Word is effectually at work in us exercising its superhuman power in those who adhere, trust and rely on it. (Ephesians 3:20, 1 Thessalonians 2:13, AMP) This is huge because it reveals that we are not called to live ordinary lives but blockbuster hits.

So our next step must be to get rid of our 'stinkin thinkin' and replace it with heaven's reality because you can't believe both. These days the world is trying to feed us an overload of negative information but you can't allow it to have priority in your thoughts and expect to live a victorious life. That's why it's imperative we do some real inside work if we are going to experience outward change. It's precisely the reason I haven't watched television for years; it takes too many withdrawals from my positive thoughts and doesn't equip me in the direction of my dreams.

I can't encourage you enough to spend quality time in conversations with God and ask Him to show you specific scriptures and promises to meditate on for your life. As you open up your Bible, there will be verses He'll point out with a heavenly yellow highlighter. Many times it will be specific individuals or character traits that He has assigned for your life. Find yourself in them. He loves to reveal and confirm your identity this way. I call these signature scriptures, and I proclaim them out loud every day. They will help you realize that God already had a magnificent plan for your life long before you or anyone else had an opinion. But ONLY to the extent that you believe who you are will you experience it.

What does your current reality say about His promises and provision in your life? Now is a good time to ask the Lord to help you see His perspective about you as a much loved child. You might be surprised at the steps He encourages you to take to draw you closer to His reality. And keep in mind, He doesn't want to point out what's wrong; He only desires to replace what's missing.

ESTABLISHED IN TRUTH

So the most vital key to reinventing your life and unlocking your greatness is to do whatever it takes to get your heart established in His TRUTH. Only then can your thoughts lead you to fulfillment and victory in every area of life. Ephesians 2:10 says, "For we are His workmanship, created in Christ Jesus for good works, which God prepared beforehand that we should walk in them." Then Psalms 139 explains that God knit you together in your mother's womb and has more thoughts of you than the numbers of the sand. That's a whole lot of thoughts!

The fact is, you are a child of the living God. You are created in His image and purchased for an elaborate price by the blood of Jesus. His DNA is pulsating inside of you, therefore; there is not an average bone in your body. The concept of average is not in God's vocabulary, nor was it ever intended to describe the existence of those He cherishes the most. You were created by an awesome God who desires you to walk into all that you already are.

> *God is not focused on fixing our behavior but winning our hearts back.*

You have got to take ownership of this reality. This is personal and you need to recognize it. God wants us to 'wear' His name boldly, like the S on Superman's chest and take hold of the colossal privileges tied to our identity. He even tells us we don't have to do anything in our own strength; that He'll create in us the power and desire we need to fulfill our call. (Philippians 2:13) My friends, we are loaded!

I spent most of my life being spoon-fed revelation about God because I had parents who were hungry to know and serve Him. They didn't just try God on for size or test the waters to see if it felt right; they went ALL IN despite how illogical it looked to the outside world. If we had the chance to do it all over again, we wouldn't have done it any other way.

However, there came a point when I wanted to be solidified in my own beliefs and experience what God had exclusively for me. Yes, there are many benefits to being raised in a Christian environment like attending church, Bible studies and being surrounded by great people, but there is always more. I discovered He longs to reveal Himself on a more intimate level.

THE SOUTHERN PRODIGAL

After leaving a corporate career, I committed to move to Colorado to attend Bible College. Immediately, God began confirming my decision in a wave of supernatural circumstances. I wasn't going to school just to receive a degree, I wanted to get as close to Jesus as possible. My mom's friend, Ann, gave me a book called Appointment in Jerusalem by Derek Prince. It's a true story of a young schoolteacher and her courageous quest to know God's will for her life. In her search for God and her life's purpose, she was led to Jerusalem.

From the moment I started reading it, the Lord began ministering to me. Situations started to arise in my life that were similar to what happened on the pages and chapters of that book. It was completely awe-inspiring. And to think this was from a story that had taken place in 1928. It was God's way of encouraging His girl that there was more to uncover.

Before leaving for Colorado, someone suggested that I read Luke 15 where Jesus is telling the story of the prodigal son to the religious leaders of the day. I wasn't sure how it would pertain to me. I was arrogantly thinking, "I'm not a wild child, I'm already seeking God and getting ready to leave everything behind for Bible College. So how in the world can this parable of a wayward, rebellious son possibly be relevant to me?" That pompous attitude should have been my first red flag. A few hours later a mentor of mine confirmed that it would be a good idea to study the story for more insight.

When I read through the account of the two brothers, God began to shine a tender light on some weaknesses that were holding me back. I related to the unruly, prodigal son squandering his time and inheritance on futile things and the other brother's pride and conceit thinking he could earn his father's love and acceptance through good behavior. As I read the story over again, it didn't produce a warm and fuzzy feeling deep inside. The good thing was that I already knew this was a story of unconditional love, restoration and redemption. One of my favorite parts is when the father says, "Son, you are always with me, and all that is mine is yours." After meditating on that, I knew I had nothing to lose but everything to gain by digging a little deeper.

God was revealing to me that I didn't have a behavior problem but an identity issue. His desire was to win my heart back in areas that I had kept from Him. If I continued to hold onto the wrong beliefs about myself and His loving kindness toward me, I would miss out on all that He had in store for the journey ahead. Once I realized that I had slipped into the world's definition of success, I did an about-face and declared that I wouldn't allow it to happen any longer. It was time for me to leave my family and my comfort zone and get back into my Father's arms. I guess you could say it was like the 'prodigal daughter' coming home so she could feast on all that her heavenly Daddy had waiting for her.

> *God's on a mission of grace and mercy to bring His children home no matter how undignified it may look.*

Then the extraordinary happened again. Two days before leaving for Colorado, my dad's secretary gave me a ring as a going away gift. The odd part was I didn't usually wear jewelry. Then, the night before I was about to leave I got a call from Kellie, a friend I'd recently reconnected with from years ago. She insisted on seeing me because she had something she wanted me to take on my journey. It filled my heart to see her since I was already getting sad about leaving. She asked me to close my eyes and put out my arms and not to open them until she said so. When she was done, I was wearing a long beautiful coat outlined with a huge fur collar and a new necklace. She had received them both as gifts but the Lord spoke clearly to her heart that she was to give them to me. When we saw the coat and then the charm that was attached to the necklace, Mom and I couldn't stop our tears. The charm was a sandal on a silver chain.

You see, in the story of the prodigal son, precisely where I'd been studying in Luke 15:20-22 (AMP), it says, "So he got up and came to his father. But while he was still a long way off, his father saw him and was moved with compassion for him, and ran and embraced him and kissed him. And the son said to him, 'Father, I have sinned against heaven and in your sight; I am no longer worthy to be called your son.' But the father said to his servants, 'Quickly bring out the best robe for the guest of honor and put it on him; and give him a ring for his hand, and sandals for his feet.'" Within two days, I had received all three of the same gifts.

It was God hugging on His girl, once again in such a way only heaven could orchestrate. Later, I discovered that in Jewish culture the robe/coat is a symbol of righteousness that deals with all our shame and wipes it away completely. The ring signifies our authority as a son or daughter and the eternal covenant with the Father that cannot be broken. The sandals represented sonship and freedom. Back then, servants were never allowed to wear shoes because they were a symbol of prestige that separated the hierarchy between the two classes.

The most beautiful part of the story of the prodigal son is the relentless pursuit of the father towards his son. It represents God's intense love toward us now and for eternity. Not only had the father been watching and waiting for his son to return but when he sees the son approaching, he runs to him with open arms. The Jewish culture considered this highly undignified. In fact, a son could be completely disowned from the family or stoned to death for squandering his inheritance or approaching his father again. This shows God the Father's unrestrained love and continual pursuit of our hearts. He's on a mission of grace and mercy to bring His children home; that is what the cross is all about.

To this day, I still get chills glancing at that coat, ring and sandal. I realize God longs for those kinds of encounters to be a part of our normal everyday experiences. In 2 Chronicles 16:9 it says, "For the eyes of the Lord run to and fro throughout the whole earth, to show Himself strong on behalf of those whose heart is loyal to Him."

That's a tiny glimpse of what the Lord had waiting for me during my two years with Him in the beautiful mountains of Colorado Springs. I was on an intentional journey in pursuit of my true identity that didn't happen overnight but it was His launching pad. Yes, I got extremely homesick, but the Lord honored my sacrifice in some incredible and humbling ways.

MIRACLE ON MONUMENT HILL

In Monument, Colorado, I stayed with a couple that agreed to host me for a month until I found a permanent place to live. The month was coming to an end and I could feel the pressure coming on. I needed some big answers and quick. Needless to say, God was faithful.

The hosting couple invited me to a neighborhood party that I had absolutely NO desire to attend. Yet something inside prompted me to go anyway. From that moment on, I have learned to listen to that internal nudge. That afternoon, I was introduced to Martie; the epitome of a sweet Georgia Peach and we hit it off from hello. Not only did she change the course of my stay in Colorado but she altered the course of my life forever.

She invited me to live with her and her husband, Jim, in their mansion on a hilltop covered with breathtaking pines. Jim was in the early stages of dementia and Martie was still traveling for her business; it worked out perfectly for everyone. The three of us became the best of friends. Jim and I built cowboy snowmen, raked leaves and he took me skiing in the hills. I helped Martie in the office and she mentored me in leadership. Whether it was shopping, movie matinees, hosting Bible studies or long walks in the piney

God wants to give you a vision to hold onto and a reality to walk into the rest of your life.

forest, we did everything together when I wasn't focused on my studies. The Siberts were my home away from home.

Not only did the Lord provide a way for me to live rent and debt free for two years but I had my own floor with an elevator! It was fully furnished with three bedrooms, two bathrooms, a living room, kitchen and porch overlooking Pikes Peak. It was like living in my own private castle. And I felt like such a princess when Martie entrusted me to drive her new pink Cadillac; nothing short of a fairytale for a small town country girl. Not only did God show up but He showed off; that's what God does.

Jim passed away before the end of my second year and during that time of transition Martie and I drew even closer. Vividly, I began to see the hand of God in my life from a much larger perspective. This wasn't about my needs being met, it was about God allowing me to serve and bless them as well. As I was embracing my identity and God's favor on my life, it allowed me to give on a more significant level. What happened in my heart and in my circumstances those two years on Monument Hill was nothing short of extraordinary. Once again I felt God's kiss.

TRUTH VS LOGIC

Learning to walk in divine favor with God and man is an integral part of your identity. A few months ago, after crawling into bed, I was thinking about God's favor over my family's life and a vision came to my heart. It was a vision of these huge heavenly arms gently laying a warm, light, fluffy blanket over me, then it tailored itself to fit my body perfectly. It brought tears to my eyes because I knew God wasn't only giving me a vision to hold onto but a reality to walk into for the rest of my days. Since then, I am learning how not to pray out of need but pray out of my identity. And believe me when I tell you, there's a big difference.

It is paramount that we get rooted in God's truths because our natural mind will stand strong and try to battle those truths with our human logic. Your mind will feed you the subtle idea that you have to change in order to please or be accepted by God. It will tell you that you need to get your act together before you can approach Him or be fully loved by Him. That is a HUGE lie and a trap; don't fall for it! I have the tendency to be performance oriented in everything; I thrive on doing well and getting results. For those of you that are the same way, you may measure your self-worth based on how well you have performed or how much you've accomplished. Living under that scrutiny can be tough. Unfortunately, we have been programmed by society to think this way. Our jobs reward us according to our performance and sometimes those closest to us give or take away their love and approval according to our deeds. This perceived expectation erodes our capacity to receive abundantly from God and keeps us locked up inside repeating the same old cycles.

There's no telling how much time I wasted thinking this way. I loved God, attended church and always knew I had a special place in His heart since I was a little girl, but I still had it backwards. For the longest time I was so focused on trying to be a 'good Christian' and work hard on fixing my flaws and shortcomings. All the while I was forfeiting precious time with Him because I felt like I needed to pull it together first. It was like trying to shovel out the darkness in a room when all I needed to do was turn on the light in my thinking. Eventually, I figured it out.

At last, I discovered that no matter how lovable we may be during our best moments, God loves us just the same as He did in our worst moment. His love and acceptance aren't dependent on us sustaining the best versions of ourselves as long as we possibly can. Nor is it about trying to create a facade of that person to those around us. The world may see what we portray but He sees us. We can't hide from God who we are and what we're about. He saw everything about us long before we were born. It's an intimate kind of knowing. He knows how we are feeling and our deepest thoughts. And good or bad, He loves us; overwhelmingly and unceasingly.

When you hold onto something that constant, it changes you. Having a permanent place to call home changes your posture as you walk out of the house and exist in this world. When you know that you have an endless wave of love to fall back on, to abide and rest in, this gives you the courage to move impossible mountains and change countless lives.

AGAINST ALL ODDS

Team Hoyt is an amazing portrayal of this exquisite kind of love alive today. Rick Hoyt, born on January 10, 1962, was diagnosed with cerebral palsy at birth after his umbilical cord became twisted around his neck. He suffered a lack of oxygen flow to his brain. As a result, his brain cannot send the correct messages to his muscles. Many doctors encouraged the Hoyts to institutionalize Rick, informing them that he would be nothing more than a 'vegetable.' His parents held onto the fact that Rick's eyes would follow them around the room, giving them hope that he would somehow be able to communicate someday. The Hoyts took Rick every week to Children's Hospital in Boston, where they met a doctor who encouraged the Hoyts to treat Rick like any other child. Rick's mother, Judy, spent hours each day teaching Rick the alphabet with sandpaper letters and posting signs on every object in the house. In a short amount of time, Rick learned the alphabet.

At the age of 11, after some persistence from his parents, Rick was fitted with a computer that enabled him to communicate and it became clear that Rick was intelligent.

With this communication device, Rick was also able to attend public schools for the first time. Rick went on to graduate from Boston University in 1993 with a degree in special education and later worked at Boston College in a computer lab helping to develop systems to aid in communication and other tasks for people with disabilities.

In 1977, Rick asked his father if they could run in a race together to benefit a lacrosse player at his school who had become paralyzed. He wanted to prove that life went on no matter what your disability may be. Dick Hoyt was not a runner and was 36 years old. After their first race Rick said, "Dad, when I'm running it feels like I'm not handicapped." After their initial five mile run, Dick began running every day with a bag of cement in the wheelchair because Rick was at school and studying, unable to train with him. Dick was able to improve his fitness so much that even when pushing his son, he was able to obtain a personal record of a 5km run in 17 minutes. They became well known on the circuit and Team Hoyt was birthed.

As of April 2014, the Hoyts have competed in 1,108 endurance events, including 72 marathons and six Ironman triathlons. They ran the Boston Marathon 32 times. Also adding to their list of achievements, Dick and Rick biked and ran across the U.S. in 1992, completing a full 3,735 miles in 45 days. For the swim portion of the triathlon, Dick uses a rope attached to his body to pull Rick sitting in a boat. For the cycle portion, Rick rides on the front of a specially designed tandem bike. For the run portion, Dick pushes Rick in his wheelchair. A bronze statue in honor of the Hoyts was dedicated on April 8, 2013, near the start of the Boston

Marathon in Hopkinton, Massachusetts, and ESPN honored Team Hoyt with the Jimmy V Perseverance Award at the ESPYS on July 17, 2013.

This is a beautiful example of an uncommon kind of love not often displayed in our world today. Rick was not capable of earning his parents love and yet they surrendered all they had to give him a quality of life that surpassed most healthy young adults. This was not a love based on behavioral modification, manipulation, merit systems or other variables we use as human beings to give or withhold our love from others. It was unconditional, overpowering and unceasing; it's what we crave but sometimes resist to give.

This is why we need to understand that Jesus didn't come to make us right, He came to make us whole. He's our safe place. It can be such a contrary picture of what we've experienced in our earthly relationships and yet it's a perfect love. Running into His arms with our weakness, struggles and mistakes is the desire of

When you know who you are, you know what you can do.

every good father's heart. Sometimes you may pour out your guts; be still in His arms, hear His voice in your heart or experience the healing power of His presence. Everything else pales in comparison to the Father's love. Restoration is the result of an intimate relationship with Him, not trying to follow a bunch of religious rules and regulations that keep us feeling defeated. You'll never hear Him say, "but I believed in you," because He never stops. He doesn't see your potential; He sees you as you really are.

The truth is, once you've received Jesus in your heart, you've already 'become' and you just need to yield to the power of God that's at work inside of you. Yielding to something that's already present is much easier than changing into something that is not. This isn't dependent on your willpower. This is called GRACE and it's the empowerment to do what you cannot do on your own.

It's just like Mr. Hoyt placing Rick in that wheelchair to push him thousands of miles on the roads, pulling him hundreds of miles in the water and bicycling for days so they could cross the finish line together. Rick knew he was a much loved son, and because he accepted and surrendered to the love of his father they experienced beautiful adventures together. They achieved the seemingly impossible that changed the world around them. Discovering the true you and walking in real identity gives you permission to be relentlessly loved despite your performance. This is freedom!

TIME TO FLY

I'll never forget, it was a nice spring day in May and I was admiring the new flowers outside the office buildings in downtown Fort Worth. While taking the elevator up in a large high-rise to prospect a customer, this reoccurring feeling overtook me. But this time it was almost unbearable. The acute awareness that I was not in the right place, at the right time, with the right people, was like being in a sci-fi movie and having an out of body experience. It was that real. The prevailing thoughts and feelings rising up on the inside were too strong to deny. I was here but supposed to be there. I didn't even consciously know where 'there' was but I knew it was somewhere I had never been. Feeling sick, nauseous and so disconnected from any sense of inner peace, I couldn't take it anymore. My job was wreaking havoc in my life. Despite the great salary, compensation, company car and expense account waiting for me, I had to walk away . . . for good this time. That day I turned in my resignation and all the things that belonged to the company. I knew I was losing a lot in the world's economy but actually, I was taking back my life. I could breathe again.

My personal beliefs had caught up with my true identity. God had a more significant call on my life, far deeper and fulfilling than material success. There was a bigger 'Yes' inside of me that needed to be given life. It was time to jump off of my map. I was not waiting on God . . . He had been patiently waiting for me to see myself through His eyes. It was time to pull out my own red cape and fly.

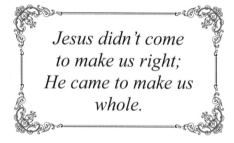

Jesus didn't come to make us right; He came to make us whole.

Begin your journey into true identity today as God is ready to reveal His signature on your life. You will release the extraordinary buried inside of you and awaken the God within. You will find yourself leaving the beaten path and aiming for the exceptional. You will begin to silence your fear and speak with your own voice. And every time you stop acting small and taking up space, you are owning your God-given identity and liberating others to follow in your footsteps. This is what superheroes do and how WE are called to exist in this world.

Come and see the view that will take your breath away!

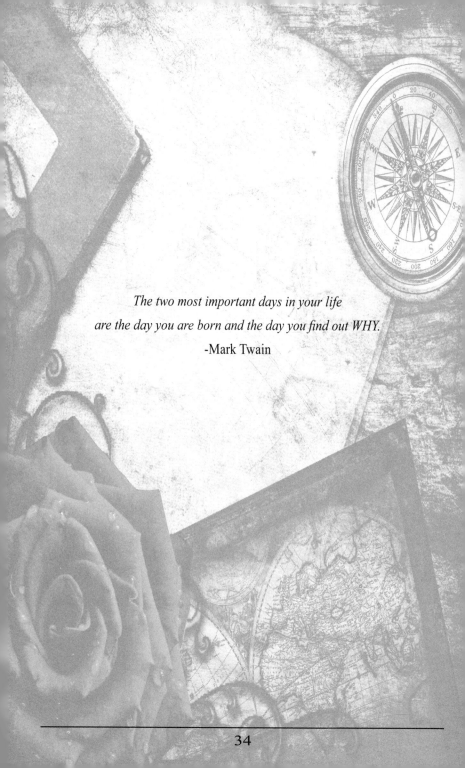

*The two most important days in your life
are the day you are born and the day you find out WHY.*
-Mark Twain

Key 2

Discover Your Echo

Discover Your Echo

It was a cold fall evening in October; I was like a kid in an outdoor candy store. We arrived at the Grand Canyon in Arizona in the nick of time to witness a breathtaking sunset. Sitting on the edge of a cliff, observing God's majestic imagination on display, was one of the most compelling moments of my life. Shouting into the sky, you could hear your voice echo through the waves of mountains. It was mesmerizing. Hearing my echo travel through space stirred up many thoughts and questions I couldn't dismiss. What is my echo in this life? What do I want to leave in this world after I am gone? Have I been living small in comparison to the call God has on my life?

I've since answered many of these questions and they've altered the direction of my life and the choices I make on a daily basis. This girl is on a divine mission and has discovered the power of living an intentional life; everything else pales in comparison.

However, I continue to meet far too many people going through the motions and daily grind of life while their hearts ache for fulfillment. Sometimes it does seem we get so busy making a living, we forget to make a life and before we know it years turn into decades. One of the greatest tragedies known to humankind is not discovering our God-given purpose, our echo. Many times life steals our passion from us and we relinquish our dreams to our personal limitations, past experiences or current circumstances. It has become too easy, especially in this age of ever-changing technology, to surrender to mediocrity and then define it as a fully lived life. Yes, random thoughts do lead to random lives; but you are anything but random! As Eleanor Roosevelt said, "Life is like a parachute jump; you've got to get it right the first time."

In a recent study, several thousand people were asked what one question they would ask God if they could be assured He would answer. The number one question, asked more times than number two and three combined, was: "What is my purpose in life?" The human heart hungers to know it exists for something bigger than itself; a much greater cause that goes beyond meeting its own needs. It's

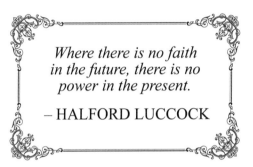

Where there is no faith in the future, there is no power in the present.

– HALFORD LUCCOCK

even been proven you can live with pain much easier than you can live without purpose. Everyone needs to have a purpose; we were created for it. And a person who hasn't discovered it is like an eagle who hasn't discovered its wings. We are born with it. It's who we are, our purpose is our unique echo and why we are here. It is how we are supposed to make our way in this world. As the saying goes, "The shame in life isn't failing to reach your dreams, but failing to have a dream to reach."

So I'm here to shout from the rooftops, "You were created for an extraordinary purpose!" And if you need me to personally come over and shout it from your rooftop, let me know . . . please just provide a sturdy ladder!

Despite your age, history or present situation, it is NEVER too late to recover your life and discover your personal Why. This is one of the primary reasons why being established in your true identity (see Key 1) is imperative and so powerful. Realizing you are KNOWN and loved by God, who is quite passionate and taken with you, will guide you and give you a specific reason for living on purpose. Jeremiah 29:11 (AMP) says, "For I know the thoughts and the plans that I have for you, says the Lord, thoughts and plans for peace and not evil, to give you hope in your final outcome." Knowing that there is a hope and a plan should encourage us not to live in vagueness but to understand and firmly grasp the will of the Lord. (Ephesians 5:17)

WE ARE PEOPLE OF PROVIDENCE

When you begin to acknowledge that you are a person of providence and not merely a coincidence, you will begin to THINK differently. You will begin to LIVE differently. Because as you discover who you are in Jesus, you will not want to be anyone else. You see, God is not all about living in the heavenlies. He's about getting down into our stuff right here, right now; living big on the inside of us. He is not an insecure, needy being expecting us to follow a bunch of dreadful rules to keep us under

> *The shame isn't failing to reach your dreams, but not having a dream to reach.*

His thumb. He is a loving Father who designed you to be fueled by a specific purpose with an endless supply of resources so you can live on full and die on empty! Nelson Mandela, said, "There is no passion to be found playing small - in settling for a life that is less than the one you are capable of living."

Now, I want to clarify, there can be a big gap between what society may call success versus true significance. Success is more about what we do for ourselves and significance is what we do for others. Significance is when you put your gifts, talents and passions into action by focusing on other people's needs. It's your sweet spot; that place where hearts are touched and lives are altered because you showed up. Significance comes in all kinds of shapes and sizes; behind the scenes and on the front lines. It could come to or through the janitor at an elementary school or the CEO of a large organization; everyone has been called to it. Unfortunately, many people have lived a life of seeming importance or experienced success but fewer have tasted significance. It should not be that way.

In the words of the late Martin Luther King Jr., "If a man is called to be a street sweeper, he should sweep the streets even as Michel Angelo painted or Beethoven composed music or Shakespeare wrote poetry. He should sweep streets so well that all the hosts of heaven and earth will pause to say, Here lived a great street sweeper who did his job well."

My question to you is, "What are you trading your life for? Are you fulfilled with your life as a whole and prospering in your sweet spot?" Is bringing value to others igniting a fire inside that can't be put out? If these questions stir up positive emotions; HOORAY! Keep reaching for the stars with your eyes on the prize; let's continue to celebrate this journey together. But if your response stirred up some negative feelings, you feel uncertain or you are totally down in the dumps or discouraged, that's absolutely okay too. You are in the right place. God is wanting to get your hopes stirred up so He can help you unpack your dreams and get on the path of a purpose driven life. Simon Sinek says, "Working hard for something we don't care about is called stress. Working hard for something we love is called passion."

START DIGGING

Whether it's being captivated by the notorious pirates Captain Kidd or Long John Silver or the cinematic heroism of Indiana Jones, most people relish a good story connected with a treasure hunt. They can be the ultimate page-turners as the characters follow a series of clues to discover the treasure of gold coins, jewelry, precious gemstones and more than enough riches to restore a hero's lost fortune. Stories can deliver thrills, adventure and possibly danger but usually there is a sense that everything will work out happily in the end. When the treasure is finally discovered, many times it represents putting things right again whether it's restoring a family fortune or saving the world from the forces of darkness.

Now's the time to stop drifting and start digging as we go on a personal quest and discover your X that marks the spot on your map of significance. The bulk of the treasure is buried on the inside of you. Indeed, it'll take some time to wipe away the layers of dust from buried dreams or hopes you've pushed aside. But rest assured, there's a bottomless treasure inside of you, waiting to be unlocked and revealed. It will take some real effort to gather the right tools, dig it up and kick in your child-like imagination, but they'll surface, I promise. In the words of Jack London, "You can't wait for inspiration. You have to go after it with a club."

Not all dreamers are winners, but all winners are dreamers.

– MARK GORMAN

So as you pick up your club, set aside any concerns about the how. The ONLY thing we are going to focus on is the what. If you have the ability to temporarily get away from your familiar surroundings and demanding schedule for a couple of days, that would be an excellent catalyst. However, if you don't have that leisure, get creative and block out some specific time every day to escape the noise of life and listen for the echo. This may seem next to impossible as you start but I guarantee you it's not. There are 86,400 seconds, 1,440 minutes and 24 hours in a day and we make time for the things that are important to us. Your life, your future and the purpose you've been called to are no small matters to be taken for granted.

When the time is right, share and communicate these necessary time adjustments to your family and friends; allow them to rally around you for help and support. It will be good for everyone and your example of focused actions might also light a flame in their hungry hearts. Even if it's just for 30 minutes to an hour each day - schedule a time to get alone with your dreams. Indeed, it takes work to quiet our souls, brainstorm and create new thought patterns after being on autopilot for so many years but the payoff is priceless. The echo of your heart will envelop you. Learning to dream again takes real commitment but once you take off the training wheels you'll realize you were created for it. Think about it, your heavenly Father is the Ultimate Dreamer desiring us to live out of our imagination not our circumstances. A man named Oriah said, "It doesn't interest me what you do for a living. I want to know what you ache for, and if you dream of meeting your heart's longing." But first you have to give your longings the opportunity and permission to be revealed and this takes time.

CALLED TO SOAR NOT SETTLE

We've all known individuals who identify and follow their life's calling with little or no effort and at times wish it could be that simple for us. This is not the majority of the population and I dare to say more people are unsatisfied than are fulfilled. Change of seasons and transitions in life can especially be challenging when we're trying to determine our place and purpose because most people tolerate their lives, they don't lead them. This is all the more reason to press on because you are not called to settle but to soar. God is a God of purpose and destiny and in the business of sharing. He is passionate about giving you a vision for your life, because a person without a future will always return to their past and there's nothing for you back there.

This is the time to ask yourself questions like: What brings you the greatest reward in life? What brings the utmost personal satisfaction? If you had no limitations (financial, relational or any other obstacles) what would you pursue that brings you joy? Why not see how far you can go, how much you can earn, how much you can share or how much you can give? What is preventing you from exploring and discovering all that you can become? Everyone's journey is supposed to be as unique as the person it is designed for. Sometimes the clues will be subtle and other times they'll be as clear as the nose on your face; but rest assured, they are there.

LOOK FOR THE CLUES

In 1975 my mom became pregnant with her fourth child. My parents were still new in their walk with the Lord but were following Him wholeheartedly. She decided she wanted a Christian doctor but had no success in locating one. Friends continued to offer her referrals but every time she scheduled an appointment she strongly felt she was making a mistake and would cancel the doctor's visit.

It sounded crazy and was against the norm at the time, yet in her heart she knew she was to deliver her baby at home; she kept it completely to herself. Days later, my dad was stepping into his closet to get dressed for work. In an instant the Lord spoke to his heart that they were to have this baby at home. Now, if you knew my dad, you'd agree this would be completely out of character for him. He's not the 'living on the edge' kind of guy. He dismissed the echo he heard.

The next day, it happened again. Immediately, he approached my mom to share what he heard and in that moment they knew God was speaking.

He spent the next day and night in a hotel room fasting and praying and decided to visit the local bookstore to browse some books on childbirth. He came across a book called *Birth without Violence* by Dr. Frederick Leboyer that validated all his thoughts and calmed his deepest concerns.

Once they made the decision to do this, the Lord gave Mom over 100 scriptures confirming their decision and revealing to her how God Himself was the 'Great Deliverer.' He promised her that she would birth in absolute peace and be a pioneer in this world. She had no idea what He was referring to in regards to the second part. Since she'd never kept a single doctor's appointment, they had no idea of her due date and she went into false labor two and a half months prior to the birth. People thought they were nuts, the inquiring phone calls were unending and there was ample opportunity for doubt and trepidation to strike. However, Mom sensed unspeakable peace and a fearlessness that were nothing short of divine. Grace was at work.

> *There are many things that catch my eye, but there are only a few things that catch my heart.*
>
> – TIM REDMOND

My brother David was born in our home on August 28th, delivered by my father. It was a perfect birth with many more miraculous events that could have only been composed by God. It wasn't until over 10 years later that Mom was introduced to the world of midwifery when a lady at church invited her to observe her home birth with a certified midwife. She spent the next two years in intense training and the next 20 years as one of God's Special Baby Deliverers; possibly one of the greatest midwives the South has ever known. Delivering over 1,000 babies with a multitude of stories, miracles and testimonies to fill a small library . . . her life is a legacy of God's faithfulness and power.

I share this story with you for two reasons. First of all, to encourage you to listen for the clues, the echoes, that may be leading you somewhere you've never traveled before, maybe even somewhere or to something you have never heard of before. No matter how foreign or unfamiliar it looks to an outsider, a flame will be kindled in front of you to take the next step onto that path or in a specific direction. Just like my parents; you have to feel the fear and entertain the doubts, but go for it anyway.

Secondly, I want you to understand that defining your purpose and uncovering your dreams can look completely different in various seasons of life. There are no absolutes but only marvelous choices that you get to make on your journey WITH the Lord. He has a multitude of options. Having my brother born at home was the catalyst that launched her into a new season of life 10 years later. Before that, Mom was a professional photographer, full-time mother and pastor. However, the next clue was revealed at the perfect time. David was their last child and the Lord was planting a seed for another season that brought clarity and served her in the years ahead. Even if Mom had not chosen that path, He would have opened up something just as extraordinary that would have suited her perfectly and touched as many lives eternally. In other words, you can't throw God off track; He always has options.

YOUR DESTINY ACCELERATORS

Now remember -- if you can imagine it, you can create it. That's why it's crucial for you to get away with your thoughts, and in this first stage do not edit your imagination. Too often we start with what is possible, but if you start there, you limit yourself and the possibilities of what you can create. God longs to cast a unique vision for your life. He'll give you some very vivid pictures for your heart backed up with principles for your head that will require you to think outside the box. Better yet, get rid of the box entirely.

This is the time to accept and receive openly all that He wants to download to you. Usually it comes through the softly spoken echo of His heart through yours. You'll realize soon enough you don't have the power to make it happen and that's how you know you're right on track. You simply need to be brave enough to jump right into the unknown and this initially starts in your thoughts. The invitation is from heaven but the eventual pursuit will be your choice. It's been said, "If the dream is big enough, the facts don't count."

Uncovering purpose also helps us refine our passions, focus our efforts and sharpen our commitments in every area of life. So at this stage of personal exploration, I highly encourage you to use some illuminating tools for your journey. Several examples would be Personality Profiles (DISC), Strengths Finder, Spiritual Gifts and the Five Love Languages assessments to name a few.

These resources provide remarkable insights into understanding yourself and others. From personality traits to love languages, character strengths, specific gifts and so much more . . . you'll see how God distinctly fulfills His purpose through people. They'll give you confirmation and clarity about your own path. And though these tools can be exceptionally accurate, they were not created to categorize or pigeonhole you but to serve you, to help you see the true you. One of my favorite quotes by Tim Redmond says, "There are many things that catch my eye, but there are only a few things that catch my heart." God already knows what will capture our hearts so we have to give Him an opportunity to get into our heads and we must do this intentionally.

It's powerful to know what captivates you, to be in alignment with your strengths and not blindsided by your weaknesses. I can attest to being on both sides. To understand what motivates you, what stresses you out and how to effectively connect with others takes loads of guesswork out of life. Someone said, "The room for self-development is the largest room in the world" . . . it's now my favorite room of the house!

Committing to a life of personal growth not only transforms your relationships but puts you on the fast track to a purpose-filled lifestyle. I call these tools destiny accelerators because they have helped me love, serve and value others better, to inspire change and to become the best I can be. Indeed, it's a lifelong excursion but there's a limitless fortune to be discovered in every soul.

FROM TOLERATION TO CELEBRATION

Almost 15 years ago my parents and I were completing a college counseling course where we were introduced to a model of human behavior. As part of the class we were required to take a DISC personality assessment and study the results. You would have thought we won the Texas lottery or struck oil! In a nutshell, what we learned enriched our lives more than any material success. For the first time in our lives we gained a real understanding of ourselves and each other's personality types. We could now understand why we act, feel and think the way we do. It provided a simple framework to guide us and gave simple strategies to connect with other people in a deeper way.

For the first time in my parents' 45 years of marriage, they moved from a place of toleration to genuine celebration. For the first time in my family's existence, we were able to breathe life into each other's needs, completely free of judgment. I truly believe that the DISC model of human behavior is the crowning information needed for relationships. I cannot image navigating a day without these principles. It lights my fire to see lives and relationships renewed and restored through this tool; especially since they lead back to The Source!

That two page assessment we took literally changed the landscape of our lives. This evaluation was also a catalyst that brought me face to face with a large portion of my destiny. Today, as an inspirational speaker and DISC Certified Master trainer, I enjoy teaching people how to build better relationships and successful lives through the model of human behavior. My heaven on earth is taking people to places they have never been or even thought possible . . . to lead them off their map and onto His. This is my happy place!

Now, it's inevitable you're going to stir up some muddy waters during your internal treasure hunt; some of this stuff has lain dormant for years. Lots of ideas are going to cross your mind but now you're learning to follow your heart. Keep digging and boldly use your imagination; it's just getting warmed up. And when your heart and imagination begin to intersect, they'll lead you to a place that common life cannot touch. This intersection will be a clue you're getting close. Excitement will start to build, your energy levels will increase and there will be little distinction whether this is work or play for you. Don't feel you need to act on every idea or thought just yet. You'll need to do some sifting and learn to evaluate new ideas. Pace yourself because this journey is not a two week excursion but a new way of life.

AN INTENTIONAL GOD LEADING YOU TO
AN INTENTIONAL LIFE

You see, those desires you're unleashing inside weren't put there by you in the first place; they were God's bright ideas. They were handcrafted and designed by an Intentional God who wants you to live an Intentional Life. He's been patiently waiting to download these things into your consciousness because He knows your feet can't go where your mind has never been. Lou Engle's quote is one of my all-time favorites, "God had a dream and He wrapped your body around it." But we have to cooperate and surrender our smallness to His bigness. And the higher you go, the more glory He receives.

A good litmus test to determine if your dreams and visions are in alignment with His is that they won't only be hard work or difficult to fulfill, but they're going to seem downright impossible. You see, that's where He lives, in the land of the impossible. Scary, of course, but that's where we get to walk off of our map and land onto His. As J.R.R. Tolkien says, "A single dream is more powerful than a thousand realities."

People close to you may think you've lost your noodles or have a few screws loose, but that's to be expected because they aren't tuned in themselves. Someone once said, "Those who dance look quite insane to those who don't hear the music."

> *God had a dream and wrapped your body around it.*
>
> *– LOU ENGLE*

To the logical mind, many things won't make any sense or the numbers won't add up on paper. Truth be told, it's not better to be safe than sorry. That's a myth that's been passed down for generations to give people a false sense of security. I would dare to say the most successful and influential people in history were the ones that took the biggest risk and 'safe' wasn't in their vocabulary.

Sir Isaac Newton once said, "If I have seen a little further it is by standing on the shoulders of giants." What if we have similar shoulders available to us? And if we do, why is it is that only a few seem to unleash their full potential like Newton did? Romans 12:2 says, "And do not be conformed to this world, but be transformed by the renewing of your mind, that you may prove what is good and acceptable and perfect will of God." We all have a gigantic set of shoulders to stand on with Father God and He is in the business of transformation. He is a Dad willing to lift us higher, show us His ways and bless us beyond our wildest dreams. Our part is to allow His reality to invade our thoughts, hearts and ultimately our lives through His Word so we can live bigger and have more impact and influence.

Those who dance look quite insane to those who don't hear the music.

God teaches us these principles through the lives of ordinary individuals who have paved the way. Our predecessors give us an invitation to use their experience as our launching pad. They've positioned us to use what they have received already so that their ceiling becomes our floor. Move forward in the clues that God provides you. This is your Father's business and you are your Father's choice. Jesus has empowered you to be an agent of change, a minister of reconciliation and a fire starter in your surroundings. Not because you 'have to go' but because you 'get to go.' This is your inheritance to enjoy.

GET COMFORTABLE GETTING UNCOMFORTABLE

A couple of years ago I was walking to my car after finishing up at the gym. While strolling through the parking lot I heard the voice of the Lord speak loudly to my heart saying, "I want you to get comfortable getting uncomfortable Tonya, that is where your destiny lies." And let me tell you something, He wasn't kidding! In that moment I decided that *yes* and *you betcha* were my new favorite responses to God, to life and to people. I had to move even when I didn't feel ready, equipped or qualified. Even if I was completely freaking out on the inside, I'd still give a confident yes. Never before have I been so stretched, uncomfortable and challenged in my life . . . and amazing opportunities and doors have opened all because of that one little word. Vincent Van Gogh said, "If you hear a voice within you say, 'you can't paint,' then by all means paint, and that voice will be silenced." I was learning to silence that voice and discovering that everything I ever wanted was truly on the other side of fear.

I compare it to watching a silent movie in black and white or living in 3D with full color and surround sound. If I had stayed snuggled up in my comfy recliner playing it safe, I would have missed out on my life. I would've missed out on an entire world God longed to open up for me.

In exchange for your comfort, the Bible says, "By the power that is at work within us, He is able to carry out His purpose and do superabundantly far over and above all that we dare ask, or think . . . infinitely beyond our highest prayers, desires, thoughts, hopes or dreams" (Ephesians 3:20 AMP). WOW, that's a pretty good exchange; I do believe we get the better end of the bargain.

THREE FEET FROM GOLD

A favorite classic of mine is the true story R. U. Darby told in Napoleon Hill's book *Think and Grow Rich*. Over a hundred years ago, Darby's uncle caught gold fever and went West to stake his claim and started digging. After weeks of hard labor, the uncle found the shining ore. He covered up his mine, then returned home to raise money to buy machinery needed to bring the ore to the surface. After collecting the money, Darby and his uncle traveled back to the site to make their fortune. They resumed digging and before long, they had enough to clear their debts and the rest would give them a massive profit. The drills went down and their hopes went up. They had discovered one of the richest gold mines in Colorado. Suddenly, the supply of gold stopped. The vein of ore had disappeared! They kept digging and drilling, but found nothing.

Deeply frustrated and disappointed, they finally quit and sold their machinery to a junk man for a few hundred dollars. The junk man decided to bring in a specialist, a mining engineer, to do some analysis. It turns out the Darbys had overlooked or were unaware of the fault lines. The junk man started drilling in the place the specialist had indicated and ...**The Gold Vein was Found Exactly Three Feet Away!** Exactly where the fault line shift indicated the gold would be. The junk man took in millions of dollars in gold ore out of the mine simply because he had the presence of mind to seek an expert (and listen to the expert) before he gave up.

The story still had a happy ending for Darby. Determined to learn his lesson from quitting early, he persevered to such an extent as an insurance salesman that he became more successful than he would have been in the gold business. He uncovered a bigger secret. He discovered the treasure inside of him could produce far more than anything on the outside.

Like Darby, you may be just three feet away from gold. On this journey seek The Ultimate Specialist as you dig and drill down to uncover your divine purpose. He knows your fault line like the back of His hand. Remember, the purest gold on the earth can be extracted less than three inches beneath your skin – your own heart. You don't have to be a miner or an Olympian to go for the gold!

THE GREATEST REWARD OF ALL

The greatest payoffs of working hard and diligently in the direction of your dreams will be the impact you have on others. You'll be contagious. God is about touching lives whether they belong to Him or not and the primary way He does this is through us. These days, action does speak louder than words. The life you lead and model will hold much more credibility than the words you use and what you speak. St. Francis of Assisi said it well, "Preach the Gospel at all times; when necessary, use words."

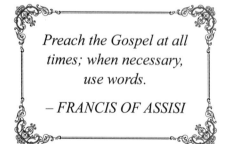

Preach the Gospel at all times; when necessary, use words.

– FRANCIS OF ASSISI

In the marketplace, mission field, at home or on a college campus, God is calling you to GREATNESS through the reality of your dreams. He's calling you through an echo to a purpose filled life. He's calling you to be a bright light in a very dark world. So unpack your dreams, stay a while and let your ECHO be heard . . . life will then be what it's meant to be!

Let Your Dreams Be Bigger Than Your Fears...
Your Actions Louder Than Your Words...
Your Faith Stronger Than Your Feelings...

Vision without execution is hallucination.

– Thomas Edison

Key 3

You've Got To Be A Termite

You've Got To Be A Termite

There are days my family asks me, "Tonya, what are your plans tomorrow?" or "What are you doing this week?" Instead of replying, "I'm working," then sharing my agenda or something of that nature, I'll say, "I'm gonna be a termite!" And they'll giggle or smile because they know exactly what I mean.

As much as I detest those little pests, they have some incredible qualities we can learn from. Do you know how a termite devours a 2x4? One bite at a time! We've all heard, it's a cinch by the inch but hard by the yard. The human eye can't detect the bite of a termite, but in one year termites do more damage to homes than fire, floods, hurricanes, tornadoes and earthquakes combined. Isn't that crazy? Such a powerful example of how small beginnings toward your dream, coupled with perseverance, truly equates to an unlimited life.

NOBODY DRIFTS TO THE TOP OF THE MOUNTAIN

I believe most people fail in the pursuit of their dreams, not because their efforts weren't good enough; most people fail because they never got started. I come across people all the time who talk about their 'big ideas' and seem to be forever preparing. They'd like to find another job, start exercising, eliminate debt, write a book . . . but they just can't seem to pull the trigger. One of the most important qualities you can develop is practicing the art of the start. As Zig Ziglar would say, "You don't have to be great to start but you have to start to be great." The power's in the takeoff, getting airborne. After you've launched you can make course corrections, but just get started. For one reason or another, people resist putting one foot forward. You'll never find the perfect time or the perfect circumstances or be totally prepared. At some point you have to kick into action. Henry Ford said, "You can't build a reputation on what you are going to do." Do not wait for someone to give you permission to begin. Nobody is going to randomly choose you, nominate you, appoint you or tap you on the shoulder and say, "Now, it's time to start." Your time is now.

Another reason people fail is because it wasn't really their desire to start in the first place; it was someone else's. This happens so often with young adults. They are ready to spread their wings and fly but instead they continue to follow the flock.

Boy, I have been there and done that! From following friends to college, to becoming a flight attendant, to pursuing a prestigious sales career; I chased after things that looked appealing to others but left me empty and unfulfilled. I would jump in with both feet, all the while knowing it wasn't my true north. Learn to listen to your heart and save yourself a few years. There's not enough passion to fan the flame when the fire is low; often it leads you to a dead end and you'll eventually quit.

Identify your purpose early on, make those decisions and then own them. In this age of instant gratification and quick fixes, we need to be reminded that our dreams won't work unless we do. Nobody drifts to the top of the mountain. Like Benjamin Franklin stated, "Well done is better than well said."

So when I say you've got to be a termite, it's encouragement to not despise small beginnings because within them lie your greatest victories. The Bible says, "He who is faithful in a very little thing is faithful also in much. And because you have been faithful in a very little thing you shall be given much." (Luke 16:10,19:17) These are priceless principles to apply in all that you do.

It's easy to sit up and take notice, what's difficult is getting up and taking action.

– HONORE de BLAZAC

Nevertheless, it is easy to get caught up in the business of life. People and daily demands start pulling us in all kinds of different directions. We lose sight of the areas where we need to be faithful the most. For example, I've been a list-maker my entire life. I'm the queen of all list-makers and a task only has about a 50% chance of happening if it's not written in my planner. I'm a busy girl. I relish checking things off, then adding more things to check off later . . . it feels so good. But beware fellow list-makers; we are called to be fruitful, NOT busy. You can spend all day being busy as a bee, thinking you are making things happen like a superhero, and still not get anything valuable accomplished.

SAYING 'NO' TO A BIGGER 'YES'

A huge, common mistake I made in the past was spending major time on minor activities that were irrelevant to fulfilling my purpose. However, everything changed once I identified my life-priorities. It is no longer difficult for me to say no to many activities because I now have a bigger YES on the inside of me. Honore de Balzac said, "It's easy to sit up and take notice, what's difficult is getting up and taking action." Once you've identified the life that God has called you to, it will be even more necessary to harness your time and proactively pursue what brings you the highest value. No longer do we have to let life happen to us. We have the freedom to plan with heaven backing up our plans. Protecting what God has put inside of us will help us stay connected to Him and the world we are called to reach. It will also help us stay focused for the long haul, not be scattered and to live with excellence.

After years of comparing myself to a termite, I discovered what John Maxwell calls The Law of Process. He emphasizes how we have a tendency to overestimate the importance of events and underestimate the power of process. Of course, we all need avenues of inspiration and motivation, whether it be from attending a conference or going to church. Events can challenge you but they don't change you. Jim Ryun said, "Motivation is what gets you started. Habit is what keeps you going." If you want to grow and see your dreams come to life, you've got to engage in a process and stay with it for the duration. More than likely it's going to require you to break some old habits and create some beneficial ones.

Maxwell's friend, Tag Short said, "The secret to your success is found in your daily agenda." I love how John Maxwell asks, "What can you see when you look at a person's daily agenda? Priorities, passion, abilities, relationships, personal disciplines, vision and influence. See what a person is doing every day, day after day, and you'll know who that person is and what he or she is becoming." *

LITTLE PEOPLE WITH BIG DREAMS

In 2005, weeks before graduating from Bible College in Colorado Springs, my parents confronted me about becoming the youth pastor for the Cowboy Church they were pastoring in Gainesville, TX. That was not exactly in line with my BIG dreams or the grand vision I pictured for my future. But in that very moment, I knew I was to say yes. I had finally figured out that God isn't as concerned about our timing as much as He is about our growth, development and obedience.

I spent almost four years with those amazing kids. They brought more joy and value to my life than I could have ever imagined. Every Sunday was Funday! My parents and I would hitch up the trailer, load up the horses and ride after breaking bread over some southern cooking. On the hour and a half drive up, we would spend time in prayer and share the messages we had prepared for church. My heart would overflow with joy

---

* The 21 Irrefutable Laws of Leadership

the second we'd pull in the parking lot and I'd see my kids. You would of thought I was leading the masses! From ages 8-18, we'd all gather in the same room of an old, small portable building, sometimes without heat, air or plumbing. And whether it was being present for them through a parent's divorce, drug addiction or teenage pregnancy; I discovered very quickly I didn't have all the answers in my toolbox. But God did, and these kids were His dream. So I knew the real journey was about them getting grounded in their God-given identity and self-worth so they could be overcomers and take their proper place in this world. That would take some time. Yet they were so eager to learn and I watched them flourish right before my eyes.

DREAM DAY

Once a month we'd have what I called Dream Day where we'd all sit in a semi-circle fashion. There were only two rules to Dream Day. The first rule was that they could have absolutely any dream they wanted or could conjure up in their imagination. It was wide open. There were no limitations or such a thing as a foolish dream; they could even change it every month. The second rule was they couldn't make fun of anyone else's dream or they'd be dismissed immediately and out the door they went. I'm telling you, we reached

Don't despise your small beginnings because within them lie your greatest victories.

so far into our imaginations that Walt Disney would've been impressed. An entire book series could've been written about our imaginary travels and the things that flowed from their creative hearts. But most of all, God changed us in that little circle. It was our favorite Sunday of the month and I'm pretty certain it was His too.

My life was altered in that old portable building because time and time again I'd experience God put His 'super' on my 'natural' through those young people. I'll never forget one particular Sunday after church when I was walking across the horse arena in that deep plowed up dirt to go saddle my horse. Just before I reached her, I heard the Lord speak to my heart and say, "Thank you Tonya, I couldn't have done this without you." I was so humbled. I realized in that moment, we were living our dreams together; God with me. Today, I'm so grateful I said yes to that four-year process. I have no doubt that being committed, at a heart level, to those kids and our growth together, literally changed history.

GET IN THE BOAT

Don't despise your small beginnings because God reveals His plans out of a growing relationship WITH Him. He's not going to give you all the steps at once; that wouldn't be faith. Indeed, He desires we all become water-walkers, so He's getting you ready for when your time comes. First, you must get in the boat that's going to take you to the uncharted waters so you can get out of the boat when He says, "Hey Tonya, (insert your name) it's time to do some water-walking!"

I've heard so many people say, "Well, I'll go when I know," but many times you won't know until you go. After all, two-thirds of God's name is GO! This is when you have to look fear in the face and leap anyway because fear is a thief. It robbed Peter of a perfectly good walk on water and kept the other 11 apostles in the boat! And it's not a matter of 'if' you mess up, but 'when' you mess up . . . be assured He will throw you a lifejacket; He's not going to let you drown. One of my favorite actors, John Wayne said, "Courage is being scared to death but saddling up anyway."

Anyone who has accomplished anything of significance has fallen on their face but they never ceased to take the next step. The step after the STING! It's the most difficult one but you must take it. It will be hard, you'll be unsure, but when your foot lands . . . oh you're going to like that feeling. We learn from the sting. If you are willing to fall, you can learn anything. Victor Kiam says, "Even if you fall on your face you're still moving forward." You can't just kind of go for it, you have to go all in. Give yourself permission to move fast and break things; it's a great way to grow.

Recently, my dad shared something with me at dinner that the Lord spoke directly into his heart. He said, "I'm available to everyone but I won't force myself on anyone." God is kind and He can only work through those who choose to be willing and open to taking action for Him. We should pray as if it all depended on God but act as if it all depended on us. At the same time, we must avoid extremes of doing nothing and feeling as though we must do everything. As God's representatives in the marketplace, in our jobs, professions and pursuits, we should seek excellence in all we do because that is His trademark. We need to recognize that people don't pay for average and God never intended us to settle for it.

Once you've established your unique purpose; then you must discipline yourself to develop it. Determine that you're going to pursue excellence while steering clear of mediocrity. This will require cultivating a lot of patience with yourself and others. Patience is grown in the gymnasium of experience and it's what rolls out the red carpet for His mercy and grace to be experienced in our life. It truly separates the good from the great; you won't go far without it. A man once prayed, "Lord, give me patience and give it to me NOW!"

For years I've dwelt and meditated on Hebrews 10:35-36 (AMP) that says, "Do not, therefore, fling away your fearless confidence, for it carries a great and glorious compensation of reward. For you have need of steadfast patience and endurance, so that you may perform and fully accomplish the will of God, and thus receive and carry away [and enjoy to the full] what is promised."

There are days I feel like a little hamster running tirelessly in circles on the spinning wheel of life; I'm going nowhere but going really fast. Other times, I realize that most of the things I put my hand to take up to four times longer than I anticipated; it can be flat out frustrating. But when I take myself back to these words in the book of Hebrews, they not only invade my soul with peace but remind me that God already knew my challenges long before I determined to take them on. Those words breathe life into my frustrations and I take another step.

> *I'd rather attempt to do something great and fail, than attempt nothing and succeed.*
>
> – ROBERT SCHULLER

Babe Ruth's condensed version of this verse might be, "You just can't beat a person who never gives up."

THE MIGHTY CHINESE BAMBOO TREE

I love reflecting on the miracle of the Chinese bamboo tree. It's a beautiful and compelling example of how this principle will work, if we adhere to it. Found in the Far East, it's a remarkable tree but different than most because it doesn't grow in the usual fashion.

Like any tree it requires water, fertile soil and sunshine for nourishment. In the first year, there are no visible signs of growth. In the second year, there are still no signs of growth above the soil in spite of providing all the right elements. The third and fourth year, still show no signs of anything happening. Then, in the fifth year, something astonishing happens. The Chinese Bamboo Tree grows 90 feet tall in just six weeks! It's almost as if you can actually see the tree growing before your very eyes.

It wasn't lying dormant for four years only to grow exponentially in the fifth year. That little tree was growing underground, developing a root system strong enough to support its potential for outward growth in the fifth year and beyond. Had it not established an unseen

Start before you are ready because there will never be a perfect time to do something that stretches you.

resilient foundation, it could not have sustained its life as it grew.

The same is true for you and me. Many of us fail to realize that pursuing your purpose is a sure thing if you just won't give up and keep watering and fertilizing the gifts inside you. The Bible says, "And let us not grow weary while doing good, for in due season we shall reap if we do not lose heart." (Galatians 6:9) Timing belongs to God but preparation belongs to us. It builds the solid character, wisdom and internal foundation to handle and sustain real success. It takes faith to work while you wait but He's got big things in store for you – some now, often times later, ALWAYS eventually.

GOD DOESN'T MEASURE TIME, HE MEASURES GROWTH

All over the world, you'll find people who've been touched by God's goodness but not changed. It's not hard inspiring people to envision their future and purposes of God. People love His promises but not necessarily the process connected to them. Real internal change is only guaranteed through the process of renewing your mind. The Bible says, "And do not be conformed to this world, but be transformed by the renewing of your mind, that you may prove what is the good and acceptable and perfect will of God" (Romans 12:2). We grow daily, not in a day. Not only are we waiting on Jesus to return but He is waiting on us to grow. He is not only preparing a place for us, but us for a place.

Yes, it requires daily discipline and your consistency is far more important than frequency. Amazingly, you will begin to crave what you feed on and your hunger for His Word will grow. Your heart will begin to beat what His heart beats for and you'll naturally recoil on the inside if your goals aren't in line with His purpose. You see, God doesn't measure time, He measures growth. His providence will unfailingly meet our preparation. As we're obedient in the space we are in right now, He opens up the next one . . . that's the power of process!

If there's one thing I've learned this past year, it is that we're never ready for growth. It's going to be new, you're going to change and you're going to be a new person. It's something that makes you feel unprepared and uncertain. If it was comfortable and easy, it

They tried to bury us, not knowing that we are seeds.

wouldn't be growth. It would be normal and standard; it would be who you already are.

Just like you're not ready for marriage, to start a family, begin a business or move to a new city; you're not ready for growth . . . and that's exactly why it will make you grow. Start before you feel ready because there will never be a perfect time to do something that stretches you. That's not a license to be reckless and to not think things through, but at some point you have to embrace the uncertainty because it is the only path forward; that's why it is called growth. All you can do is step into it with everything you've got. Nelson Mandela said it this way, "It always seems impossible until it's done."

FOR SUCH A TIME AS THIS

Many years ago the Lord led me to the book of Esther. It's the story of an ordinary girl who fulfills an extraordinary challenge in an unlikely situation. It's been the most influential book in the Bible for me. Not only has it reinforced my identity and passion but it's empowered me to commit to the process of purpose and purity. The story is beautifully portrayed in the movie, One Night with the King based on the book Hadassah by Tommy Tenney and Mark Olsen. I've worn out my personal DVD copy and yet I am more fascinated every time I watch it.

As an orphaned Jewish child, Esther was taken under the wing of her older cousin Mordecai who served in the Persian ruler's palace. Being groomed and prepared at an early age, she remained submitted to his wisdom and instruction. Because she maintained a teachable spirit she grew up knowing who God called her to be and the favor of the Lord was all over her.

Years later, she was taken captive by the king's court along with the other most beautiful virgins in the land. Eventually the king would personally select one to become his queen. They were required to go through a stringent 12 month preparation period before they could even approach the king. After meeting the specific requirements for a full year, the women were given the opportunity to take anything they desired with them to the palace when the big day finally arrived.

As a former orphaned peasant girl, Esther could have easily gotten caught up in the pageantry, fame of royalty or gone the other way and rebelled against authority. Not only did she remain humble and committed to the process, she found unprecedented favor during her entire time of captivity. The Bible said Esther obtained favor in the sight of all who saw her. Her heart belonged to God which ultimately led her into the arms of the king. She embraced God's plan and was compelled to act on it while keeping her Jewish heritage hidden. As his chosen queen she held a significant place of influence that grew deep in the Persian Empire.

Then God's providence and Esther's preparation would meet again. Mordecai (Esther's cousin) refused to bow down and pay homage to Haman, a high official of the king. Haman became infuriated and plotted to destroy all the Jews in the kingdom because of his pride. Mordecai heard of the plot and reported it to Esther saying, "For if you remain silent at this time, relief and deliverance will arise for the Jews from another place and you and your father's house will perish. And who knows whether you have come to the kingdom for such a time as this?" (Esther 4:14)

Esther outwits Haman and takes her petition to the king and pleas for the protection of her Jewish people from Haman's wicked strategy. The king, out of anger, has Haman hung on the gallows which he had built to destroy all the Jews. Esther's faith and courage saves her people.

Esther is clearly a story of God's intervention and deliverance. She was a woman of principle who was willing to put the lives of others before her own. All those years of preparation were not wasted but set her in a position to save the Jewish nation and ultimately protected the lineage of the coming Messiah. She took possession of her God-ordained vision despite the great risk and her choices changed world history.

Many times our lives seem pretty routine, but all of us have a few defining moments when we are called upon to put godly principles above personal benefit. Winston Churchill described it like this, "There comes a special moment in everyone's life, a moment for which that person was born. That special opportunity, when he seizes it, will fulfill his mission – a mission for which he is uniquely qualified. In that moment he finds greatness. It is his finest hour."

What will you do when you encounter those defining moments in your life? What will you do when you face a 'such a time as this' moment? Will you choose to do the right thing as opposed to what might give you some personal benefit?

Learning to discern the right action for the right time is what brings success in all of our lives. And when we act on God's Word, He goes to work behind the scenes. Devoting yourself to the process provides you with practical experiences and courage to seize opportunities that lead to greater risks and larger victories. You were undeniably born into the kingdom for such a time as this; seize your finest hour.

CHAMPIONS DON'T BECOME CHAMPIONS IN THE RING

Sports have always been a big part of our family's world; competition is in our bloodline. I believe the day each of us Spence babies exited my mother's womb, we headed straight to the sporting goods store to get fitted for our softball, soccer, volleyball, basketball and, of course, golf equipment! Dad has always been our favorite coach, teaching us so many life lessons through the games. Today, my siblings and I still relish playing, coaching and helping others improve their skills through the love of these games. It's such a great way to build self-confidence and character.

Every great athlete knows you can have all the natural gifts, talent and potential one person can hold, but you've got to be committed to the daily

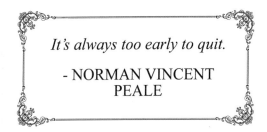

It's always too early to quit.

- NORMAN VINCENT PEALE

discipline, hard work and grind to actually excel. If not, you can be beaten by someone with less talent but more tenacity and dedication to becoming a champion. It's the blood, sweat and tears that separate the good from the great.

We should all aim to be our best and finish well in our life pursuits. Live by the words of Norman Vincent Peale who said, "It's always too early to quit." As we persevere, our confidence will be rewarded and our obedience will be recognized. But don't get discouraged if it seems delayed. Our journey is not a sprint but a marathon and we must pace ourselves to endure to the end.

There's an old saying, "Champions don't become champions in the ring – they are merely recognized there." It's all in your daily routine. Former heavyweight champ Joe Frazier said, "You can map out a fight plan or a life plan, but when the action starts, it may not go the way you planned, and you're down to your reflexes -- that means your preparation. That's where your roadwork shows. If you cheated on that in the dark of the morning, well, you're going to get found out now, under the bright lights."

Hold tight to the Law of Process and relish its rewards along the way. Decide today you're going to enjoy and appreciate your own journey; it will build character traits to serve you the rest of your life. And the next time somebody asks you what you're going to do, tell them, "I'm gonna be a termite!" and take another bite out of that 2x4!

Walking off Your Map

It's not who you believe in that changes your life forever, but who believes in you.

Key 4

Your Company Is Contagious

Your Company Is Contagious

"You got this Spence, just give it a little more Wheaties!" he would holler from the sidelines. The image of those tender eyes and that special warm smile gleaming from a thick beard will be engraved on my heart forever. His name was Marshall. He was my softball coach for a couple of seasons while playing on the 'big girls' team. My primary position was pitcher but sometimes I'd hit a slump and it seemed like nothing could pull me out . . . except Marshall. He had this uncanny ability to make me believe I was still the best, even at my worst. He wouldn't even give me permission to mope or get down on myself when it felt so justified. I don't recall the exact words he'd say in our huddle but it was more about how he made me feel. He'd squeeze my shoulder with his grizzly hand while telling me all the things I did right and say, "We'll get 'em next time champ!" The funny thing is, I knew it was coming straight from his heart and it would land right in the middle of mine; just when I needed it the most.

For years I thought that if I worked hard, improved my skills and did the right thing; I'd be successful and happy. These are essential traits for success but I took for granted a timeless key that is irrefutable in all our lives. John Maxwell calls it the Law of The Inner Circle. That is, your potential is determined by the ones closest to you because you become what you're around.

Have you identified the 'Marshalls' in your life? Those relationships that genuinely celebrate you, longing to see you shine yet know how to peel you off the ground when you've fallen flat on your face. The ones that wrap your wilted arms around their shoulders when all your strength has vanished and you feel there's nothing left. Those are the friends that drag you across the finish line no matter how sweaty, stinky or bloody you've gotten because they are there to see you win. You need to identify, relish and nurture these people in your world . . . they are your lifeline!

LET CURIOSITY BE YOUR COMPASS

Both of my parents modeled very pioneering lives. They have blazed legendary trails for many to follow in the horse industry, ministry and midwifery. Still believing their best years are yet to come they are committed to re-firing not retiring. Being raised in that environment has shaped and empowered me to believe in the beauty of my dreams; even when those dreams changed every other day.

In our younger years, when my sister, Tammy, and I decided we wanted to pack up and live with the wild Indians, Mom bought the outfits and painted our faces while Dad built the tee-pees and composed our Indian names. We joined a group called Indian Princess and went all out in our tribal ventures. Another year, I yearned to be a professional rodeo clown. To my surprise, my parents arranged a week-long trip for me to travel the west Texas rodeo circuit with a professional bullfighter and his wife. They were precious friends of ours, but indeed, my desires changed quickly. After witnessing the painful injuries and living out of a small camper for seven days, I determined the need to come up with plan B.

Motion pictures could be filmed about the adventures of me and my siblings through the years. Of course, my parents walked in wisdom and would be the voice of reason but we never heard things like: You can't do that; That doesn't make any sense; You're not smart enough, or gifted in that area. Expressions of discouragement were never spoken under our roof. We grew up believing . . . in ourselves and each other.

I'm forever grateful my parents inspired us to live out of our imagination and curiosity. Logic wasn't always the primary compass in our lives but the voice of God in our hearts guided our steps. Did we fall, mess up and waste some precious time and money? Of course we did and there are times I still do to this day.

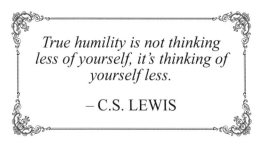

True humility is not thinking less of yourself, it's thinking of yourself less.

– C.S. LEWIS

Being embraced by people who believe in you despite your shortcomings, builds tenacity and makes you relentless. Our parents modeled purpose-driven lives, fueling a flame to press on that far surpassed logic. We learned that there is no failure in life unless you give up, but that was never an option. We would just say, "Next!" It wasn't until my adult years that I understood the gravity of this principle because, fortunately, Mom and Dad had made it our normal.

THE AVERAGE OF THE FIVE

So my question to you is this, "Who's rubbing off on you?" What kind of impact are the ones closest to you having on your attitude and life? Have you ever noticed that you begin to talk, act and think like the people you hang out with the most? You begin to use the same phrases, finish each other's sentences or even pick up their mannerisms. My mom and I are best friends; she is my ultimate she-ro. I can't tell you how many times, without saying a word, we can look at each other and know exactly what the other is thinking. It's crazy! Or I'll want her opinion on something, yet I usually know her response before even asking. That's because we've spent so much time together.

Jim Rohn puts it this way, "You are the average of the five people you spend the most time with." Now, I realize that's a big statement to digest as you imagine your own circle of friends, and it's even more difficult to act on. But what if those relationships are truly the window into your future? This is serious stuff. I'm not suggesting that we should abandon all of our current relationships and exchange them for new ones so we can pretend to be something we're not. What I am encouraging you to do is honestly examine their influence in your life. Which ones are positive and which ones are negative?

One of the most challenging adjustments people face when walking off of their map and into their destiny is letting go of destructive relationships. I'm referring to the ones that so eagerly express their disapproval and try to devour your hope. It doesn't matter how smart, qualified and intelligent you are . . . if you allow negative, fearful people into your inner circle; they will get into your head. Not only will they impact the way you see

Keep and guard your heart with all vigilance.

– PROVERBS 4:23

yourself and experience the world around you, they're often the determining factor if you will walk into ultimate success or failure. You can't hang out with negative people and expect to live a positive

life. Choose to be with people who call you up to a new level; not hold you down to an old one as you try to grow.

WHEN WORDS AREN'T ENOUGH

For years my dad has shared this story with us from God's Little Devotional Book and it moves me every time. While doing research for a doctoral thesis, a young man spent a year with a group of Navajo Indians on a reservation in the Southwest. He lived with one family, sleeping in their hut, eating their food, working with them and generally living their life. The grandmother of the family spoke no English, yet a very close friendship formed between the grandmother and the doctoral student. They seemed to share the common language of love and they intuitively understood each other. Over the months, he learned a few phrases of

Navajo and she picked up words and phrases in English.

When it was time for the young man to return to the university and write his thesis, the tribe held a going-away celebration for him. It was marked by sadness since he had developed a close relationship with all those in the village. As he prepared to get into his pickup truck and drive away, the old grandmother came to tell him goodbye. With tears streaming from her eyes, she placed her hands on either side of his face, looked directly into his eyes, and said, "I like me best when I'm with you."

True friendship is letting those around you not only 'be themselves' but 'be their best.' Remember, people know what you are by what they see, not by what they hear.

The entire book of Proverbs is chock-full of wisdom for life and relationships. It says, "He who walks with wise men will be wise, but the companion of fools will be destroyed. Keep and guard your heart with all vigilance, for out of it flow the springs of life." (Proverbs 13:20, Proverbs 4:23)

The best 'heart guard' on the market is surrounding yourself with people who are optimistic, encouraging, loyal and authentic. Spend time with those who make you happy not with those you have to impress. One of my favorite quotes by Wilfred Peterson is, "Walk with dreamers, the believers, the courageous, the cheerful, the planners, the doers, the successful people with their head in the clouds and their feet on the ground. Let their

You are the average of the five people you spend the most time with.

– JIM ROHN

spirit ignite a fire within." These are the people you want in your tribe.

And never forget, God will always be your biggest fan. He believes in you and the reality of your dreams far more than anyone else; including you! He's the one responsible for dropping them in your heart from the get go, with a million bright ideas on how to make this happen. Why not let Him be your first place of refuge, encouragement and wisdom? He's so good at it.

It's been said, "If you're the smartest person in the room, you're in the wrong room." Great point, but the truth is, HE'S ALWAYS IN THE ROOM! We just need to acknowledge His presence, put our ears up to His heart and listen to what He has to say. He is brilliant!

THE IRRESISTIBLE EXAMPLE

God's desire is for us to keep our eyes on heaven while loving each other here on earth. One of the noblest ways to do this is to simply love sincerely and live by example. We need to live out our convictions with integrity without imposing them on others. If you stay true to what God has called you to do and be content with the areas He has asked you to surrender to, your life will begin to align in such a way that others will long to experience the peace you exude.

> *Nothing is more confusing than those who give good advice and set a bad example.*

If your friend struggles with alcoholism, be his anchor not his temptation. If your friend is in an impure relationship, don't judge, just love them and honor their free will. Let's be honest with each other about our ethics and ideals and theology without expecting people to change because we feel like they should. It's time for Christians to walk in the same unconditional love and acceptance that was granted to us; how dare we withhold what was so freely given to each of us.

Everyone knows it's much easier to talk about what's right than to do what's right. And nothing is more confusing than watching those who give good advice but set a bad example. On the other hand, there is nothing that is more convincing than living out what you say you believe in with steadfast integrity. I can remember the day that I decided that I would not teach anything I did not try to live out. As a youth pastor, I wanted my words to hold weight. I knew trying to teach something I wasn't living was a dead end road when it came to reaching their hearts. I'll admit, it humbly narrowed my options but it simultaneously empowered me to step up as a leader and be more transparent in my own struggles. Those kids watched me like a hawk. Quickly, I learned they might doubt what I say but they easily believed what I did and they imitated it.

We need to be a catalyst of hope. It's in that space that we create an atmosphere where people desire to follow our leading. We aren't called to be drill sergeants that command, but role models that convince. As John Maxwell puts it, "Too many leaders are like bad travel agents. They send people places they have never been. Instead, they should be more like tour guides, taking people places they have gone and sharing the wisdom of their own experiences."

REDHEADS AND ANGELS

I'll never forget that cold, rainy evening back in January when our church was starting off the year with 21 days of early morning worship and prayer. My heart longed to make the valor commitment to attend, but as a night owl I completely resisted. Finally, I told the Lord, "If you'll wake me up without setting the alarm clock, I will go." Well, you can guess what happened next. He woke me up, every morning.

Those 21 days in His presence were priceless. But the most sobering moment was on the fourth morning when I noticed a little, pale-skinned, red-headed girl, about six or seven years old. She was boldly pacing the auditorium and praying with her hands lifted in the air. My first thought was, "She must be following her mom." But there was not an adult near and I couldn't keep my eyes off her. She was so consumed in worship, talking to God and it looked as if He was talking right back; she was so engaged. She wasn't concerned about how she was going to pay her bills, relationship issues, sickness or stressful circumstances. She wasn't there to impress her peers or battle a mental *To Do* list. She wasn't there to earn God's acceptance or learn a bunch of principles to live by. She was just a child loving her God with all her heart and He was obviously loving her right back.

Tears escape when I think of that little red-head. She's a vivid reminder that this is what I was created for; to be my Daddy's girl and continually bask in His relentless love. No wonder God refers to us as His children all throughout the Bible. He never intended us to carry such heavy loads alone. He longs to provide for us and love on us as any great father would do. And though we deserve nothing, He still gives us everything.

In Mathew 18:4-5 Jesus said, "Whoever humbles himself as this little child is the greatest in the kingdom of heaven. And whoever receives one little child like this in my name receives me." Your job, your dream, your spouse, your accomplishments, your family and friends, your bank account . . . should not be your ultimate source of fulfillment. Having an intimate relationship with your heavenly Father . . . this is where it's all at!

In 1981 my dad worked out of a small office in downtown Keller, Texas. My mom and sister, Dondi, who was six years old at the time, stopped by to chat with Dad and friends on the way home. They were all gathered around Sandy's desk in the receptionist area when Dondi started tugging on Mom's sleeve trying to interrupt her. Finally, Mom acknowledged her and Dondi said, "There's an angel over there." Immediately Mom dropped everything and asked her where. By the look on my sister's face she knew this was not made up; Dondi was not a child into pretending or having imaginary friends.

Once again, Mom asked her where the angel was and she pointed about 10 feet away to the dark paneled wall, close to the door. Mom asked if she could still see it and she said yes. A couple minutes later she said he went straight up through the ceiling. She genuinely described the angel as being tall, almost to the ceiling, wearing white with blonde hair. Dondi never mentioned having a conversation or hearing any verbal words spoken but she intuitively knew, without question, that this was her guardian angel. In Mathew 18:10 Jesus said, "Take heed that you do not despise one of these little ones, for I say to you that in heaven their angels always see the face of My Father who is in heaven." Today, my sister will tell you she has a difficult time remembering any details but it was more about the feeling of his peaceful presence.

No wonder God asks us to come to Him as little children. He's longing to interrupt us with something astounding but we are often too distracted to take notice. Some days we just need to remember; we aren't gathering around a scripture, a belief or a doctrine but we are gathering around our Father.

> *God wants to hear and talk about what we are born for; not what we are programmed to pray for.*

Indeed, life gets busy but if our childlike peace begins to diminish maybe it's time to spend a little time with Dad and let His love rub off on us.

Now don't get me wrong, I do believe principles are an intricate part of living successfully; they were created for our benefit. However, don't make the mistake of forfeiting God's presence over His principles in any part of your life. When we are overly devoted to principles or systems, we'll get to where we don't need Him to show up because He will always honor those principles. But when we learn to walk in His presence, more stuff will happen by accident than when we try to make them happen on purpose. He's all about relationship not religion. For example, He doesn't like hearing what we have been programmed to ask and pray for, He wants to hear and talk about what we were born for. If you have a hard time hearing from the Lord why don't you talk about some things He wants to talk about; like the mark He's called you to make on this world.

So this is not about church on Sunday, joining a Bible study, attending a motivational seminar or ongoing personal development . . . this is about your journey with your God. It's about daily Father/daughter and Father/son moments that take your breath away. This is what you were created for.

BE CONTAGIOUS

And I saved the best for last! The most powerful part of this key is who you become in the process of allowing positive influences and people to rub off on you; especially your heavenly Father. You'll be like my Coach Marshall in somebody else's world when they need it the most. This is when we get to join people as they push past the thresholds of what they thought they were ever capable of. You'll see in others what they don't see in themselves and due to their interaction with you; they'll wonder how they could've missed it! With every person I encounter, I love to play what I call The Seek and Find Game. I seek out their greatness and I ALWAYS find it. Once you start engaging in this personal game, it will become second nature and you'll experience the impact for yourself. Destinies will be changed because God revealed His reality of someone through YOU. It's like they can see into the mirror of their perfection. Now that's what I call living!

We need to be reminded that love looks like something; it doesn't just say something. We keep trying to explain God's love to people and He is wanting them to encounter Him through us. God is looking for friends with hearts yielded and willing to say YES . . . yes to the echoes and whispers He speaks to us. Yes to love others how Jesus loves. Yes, no matter what the costs may be. It's not that complicated; just live on behalf of the one who has given you His everything.

So, let's do a quick exercise. Imagine a short, chubby boy who is a little on the clumsy side. He shares with you his big dream of becoming an NBA basketball player for the Boston Celtics. How are you going to respond to that? "Son, I suggest you quit watching so much television and replace it with a gym membership, cut back on the ice cream and find yourself another dream, real quick." No, no, no, don't you dare! You should simply encourage him to find a good coach, practice hard and learn how to jump high, REALLLLLLLLY HIGH!

Or let's say a young, poverty-stricken girl with little or no education has aspirations of being a movie star. How are you going to handle that one? Immediately, you look her straight in the eyes, with anticipation in your face and say, "Girl, I can see it now! It's Friday night and my friends and I have arrived at the theater. We're all ready for some action and buttery popcorn. We walk up to get our tickets and there's your picture in full size on the billboard's Top 10 Box Office Hits. You have the starring role on the big screen. After the movie's over, the credits begin to roll and I see your name again. I got so excited because I knew you accomplished your dream and I get to tell all my friends, I know that girl!"

The next thing you can do as you encourage her is to pull out a piece of paper and a pen and ask for her autograph. When she asks you why, you tell her, "Because I just know one day you're going to be famous! There's absolutely nothing you can't do when you put your heart and soul into it."

Then encourage her to start looking into drama classes at her school or local church, to read acting books and find someone to give her guidance.

And these, my friends, are small examples of this powerful key. Intentionally surround yourself with the positive influences you're aspiring to. Believe in others more than they believe in themselves. It's simple; just love Jesus and the one in front of you! Destinies will be altered right before your very eyes . . . including your own.

> *When you stop chasing the wrong things you give the right things a chance to catch you.*
>
> – LOLLY DASKAL

It is not happy people who are grateful, it is grateful people who are happy.

Key 5

Turning Madness Into Gladness

Turning Madness Into Gladness

I f I had to choose the two most important words in the English language, they would be *thank you*. They're the first two words I express to the Lord in the morning and last ones conveyed from my heart at night. Every day is a gift we should be grateful to unwrap.

With all the darkness and destruction taking place in humanity today, it's not difficult to lose sight of what's going right because there is so much wrong. Turning madness into gladness is about cultivating a deep attitude of gratitude, at the core of your being, despite what is going on in the world around you. It vastly improves your quality of life and will take your relationships to new heights.

You'll discover, if you haven't already, that pursuing your dreams can create some very maddening moments. Whether it be a series of unexpected circumstances or a verbal assault from someone you love, stuff will happen. How

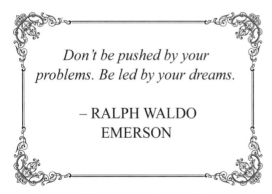

Don't be pushed by your problems. Be led by your dreams.

– RALPH WALDO EMERSON

you've conditioned your heart will determine if you respond in a positive way or react in a negative one. Ralph Waldo Emerson said, "Don't be pushed by your problems. Be led by your dreams." Our heart's condition will determine which of these paths we'll go down.

THE LAW OF POLARITY

The universal law of polarity says everything has an opposite (example: hot/cold, up/down, positive/negative). However, you can only focus on one polarity at a time. You cannot be both positive and negative; you are either one or the other. This is important to understand because you get to choose.

The Bible says, "Enter into His gates with thanksgiving and into His courts with praise." (Psalms 100:4) This is how our heavenly Father requests we approach Him and there's a valid reason for this. He knows the power of a positive heart. When we are pursuing a new level in life, we can accelerate the process by drastically increasing our heartfelt gratefulness; it's the sign of a flourishing soul. We learn to love Him all over again, and again, and again.

The Bible also says, "Be anxious for nothing, but in everything by prayer and supplication, with thanksgiving, let your requests be made known to God." (Philippians 4:6) I don't know about you, but every time I read the word, 'nothing' in that scripture, I do a double take. Nothing means nothing! I know God's literal about what He says here, but isn't this pushing it a little far? I've got a lot on my plate, some big challenges staring me in the face and some worry is to be expected, right? The answer is no. He doesn't want us to worry about a single thing. He tells us to take our problems back to the promises; not to friends, family or peers. Hearing contradicting advice brings confusion not clarity, so we are first and foremost to seek His wisdom. Then, to top it off, He reminds us that our only part is to be thankful and let Him know what we need. Don't worry if you don't feel like you can't get to God, He will get to you.

THE HIGHS, THE LOWS AND THE IN-BETWEENS

In the moment of your deepest need, you need to encounter God's peace and be receptive to His wisdom. When you've been abiding in thanksgiving it is much easier since you are directly tuned into His channel. But when you've been trapped in the dungeons of deep despair, it's much more difficult to dig yourself out if you haven't learned to connect with Him during the highs, the lows and the in-betweens.

As God's children we must learn to fight from a position of offense and victory; not towards it. Jesus has already won the war. That is enough to be grateful for every day! In reading the accounts of Jesus through the Scriptures, you don't see Him addressing the problems. He just brings the solutions. His posture, power, predisposition and providence were always greater than any problem coming at Him. We must live with the conviction that nothing is impossible with God and not allow the problem to become larger than the solution. Live with a conviction that today is a great day for a miracle, regardless of how many times you have personally prayed for it.

We are more than conquerors because we know the results before we even enter the fight. We are not overcome by negative circumstances; we are strengthened

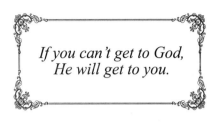

If you can't get to God, He will get to you.

by His faithfulness in our lives. Do whatever it takes to get this from your head and engrave it on your heart. Pull out your lipstick or shaving cream and write on your bathroom mirror, make it your cell phone wallpaper . . .you are more than a conqueror!

FROM DREAM TO NIGHTMARE

Back in 2002, my mom, sister and I went ice skating with friends from a local church. It had been years since any of us had set foot on ice. We all started out slow, holding each other up because we were laughing so hard after pulling each other down; it was a riot! After the first few laps, I got my groove back. My speed went up as my timidity went down. My confidence was rising high. It wasn't long before I had visions of the elegant, black sequined, feathered costume I envisioned wearing for the upcoming figure skating competition at the Winter Olympics. However, just a few minutes later, my vivid dream became an ugly nightmare. The sweater I had tied around my waist came loose, went under the blade of my skate and threw me off balance. There was no way to stop; I was going much too fast. I flew forward and crashed hard on my right shoulder. The couple next to me said it was a terrible blow and instantly figured it would be a bad break.

Immediately, they cleared the rink, carried me into the dressing room and located a doctor in the building. I was in so much pain I could hardly breathe and I remember getting colder and colder from the shock. After following some of the doctor's instructions and answering a couple questions, he told Mom they needed to get me to an emergency room right away. My arm was definitely broken; if not something worse.

Well, this was my opportunity to look to Jesus as being bigger in my life than the problem I was facing. What was amazing was I had been digging into scriptures about healing weeks prior to the accident. Through teaching CD's, meditating on the scriptures and God's track record in my own life, my heart was established. I was certain of the finished work of Jesus as my healer. Mom knew this but had to be brave. After they loaded me up in the truck, she looked at me square in the eyes and said, "Tonya, what do you want us to do? Do you want us to take you to the hospital or take you home?" Without hesitation I said, "Take me home." The moment I released those words out of my mouth, I knew healing was mine. My faith was stronger than my pain and there was no looking back.

My parents got me in bed, prayed until the pain subsided and I finally fell asleep. A few hours later I woke up screaming in excruciating pain and couldn't stop the tears from flowing. Dad and Mom prayed but also asked if I wanted to go the hospital. I said, "No, just keep praying," and I started speaking the Word out loud over my body. In less than an hour, the pain completely stopped and I fell sound asleep. The next morning the Lord gave me a scripture to stand on as I could feel a slight twinge in my shoulder. It said, "Many evils confront the consistently righteous, but the Lord delivers them out of them all. He keeps all his bones; not one of them is broken." (Psalms 34:19-20 AMP) I was so excited when I received that verse. I knew it was straight from His heart to mine. Within three days my arm was totally healed with no pain or residual effects; God is so good! He turned my madness into gladness!

THE BIG TWO

It's inevitable that we're all going to face challenging situations; they're presented to us daily; sometimes hourly. Yes, we need to be strong and it's good to offer a sense of security to the ones around us. At the same time, we need to resist the temptation to sugarcoat things or pretend everything is okay when others know it really isn't; there's a fine line. We must practice being honest and authentic with God, ourselves and others in order for our lives and relationships to flourish. God will always help you find a way out of your circumstances but the most important thing to Him is that He wants to find a way into your heart. When things get tough, I get away with Him and then my faith arises when I simply hang out with the Faithful One.

So when stuff happens, refuse to be offended with God. Use any loss to fuel your fire. Don't let yourself live by your experiences; they only pull the Gospel down to that level. Instead, set the Gospel as your standard and let it pull your life up to its level. Get back on the front lines and go looking for the next impossibility to bow its knee to Jesus.

Get wisdom from the Word about your situations and pour your energy into the things you can control; not what you can't. Fretting over the economy, people's decisions and other uncontrollable factors is a waste of time and energy. The only things you need to focus on

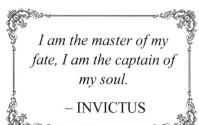

I am the master of my fate, I am the captain of my soul.

– INVICTUS

are the TWO things you can control; your attitude and your effort. You can choose to wake up and meet the day with a positive outlook and anticipation of good things to come. You can decide to treat others with dignity and respect while giving your best in everything you do. Let 'the big two' be your best allies in times of trouble. They will serve you well.

A VOICE IN THE STORM

In 2000, my brother David was working for a government agency as a research fisheries biologist based in Hawaii. It would be his first trip at sea with ample opportunities for anxiety and fear to take root. Living with the bare necessities right out of college, he was far removed from family with his first baby born just months prior to his departure from Texas. Unfortunately, he had no inkling of when he would return.

With a Korean captain and four Filipino men as crew, David was the only English speaking crew member on board the approximately 80-foot long liner tuna boat. On first site of the worn down, beaten vessel, David's heart sunk and fear started knocking at his door. It was a similar boat to the one used in the movie *Perfect Storm*. The bathroom consisted of a five-gallon bucket and no matter how sick you got, there was no turning back. Traveling up to 1,000 miles into the Pacific Ocean, they hit high seas shortly after departure. It was a tough voyage where they would only see the sun for one day out of the entire 23-day journey.

Sure enough, seasickness struck David full on the very first day, making him terribly nauseous and unable to function. Remarkably, back home in Southlake, Texas, Mom woke up in the middle of the night to use the restroom. For the first time in her life she experienced intense vertigo which is comparable to feeling seasick. Becoming extremely nauseous and barely able to stand, the Holy Spirit prompted her to pray for David. Later, we discovered it was on the exact day and time his sickness had occurred. After retiring to the bunk, he didn't wake up for over 24 hours but was completely rested and restored. Despite the raging winds and violent seas, he never experienced a trace of sea sickness again.

When loneliness and fear offered to be his closest companions, David chose to seek God. In the midst of the storms, he would read his Bible and spend time in prayer and study, feeling God's presence in the darkest of nights. It was almost tangible.

The days were long and the work was grueling. David was also responsible for taking measurements and biopsies of the sharks, tuna, marlin and other wild species they caught; it was risky business. As much as possible, the crew tried to steer clear and work away from the 30-mile long line that ran across the deck. It was like a cable running in an L shape on the boat. If it snapped, the force would be so powerful it could be extremely dangerous, if not deadly. Though it wasn't a common occurrence, many crew members who'd been around awhile fell victim to its blow. Countless men had missing fingers, ears, were blinded or displayed scars from injuries due to this cable.

One late evening while pulling in fish, David was having to work next to the big line. Suddenly, a strong, compelling voice on the inside said, "Move out of the way!" He rushed to another part of the deck. Within seconds, the line completely snapped where he was standing, sounding off like a shotgun. David knew his life had just been spared by the voice of God in his heart. He said it was so audible it was difficult to distinguish it from the voice of a person speaking right to him.

This reminds me of the wonderful story of Jesus with his disciples in Mark 4:35-41. After teaching a large crowd of people, Jesus instructed His disciples to get into the boat and cross over to the other side of the sea. Jesus was fully God, but on earth He also functioned as 100% man. He only did what the Father instructed Him to do. In this passage He had been walking long distances, teaching and healing hundreds of people so He must have been exhausted. He went back to the boat, laid His head on a cushion and fell asleep.

Many of the disciples in the boat were professional fisherman. They had been in many storms before, but this one frightened them. The waves were breaking into the boat, so the boat was filling up with water. They probably did everything they knew to do before waking up Jesus. By the time they went to Him, they were terrified and thought they were going to drown.

Then the Bible says, "Jesus arose and rebuked the wind, and said to the sea, 'Peace, be still!' And the wind ceased and there was a great calm." To the disciples' amazement, Jesus only had to speak a few words and the storm became silent. The wind stopped and the water was still. He spoke and the sea obeyed. The storm's obedience to Jesus' command gave further proof that Jesus was God! When the disciples FINALLY called on Jesus, He brought peace where there had only been chaos.

> *God doesn't want us to pull Him into our storms; He desires to draw us into our peace.*

My brother knew it wasn't just him and those five crew members aboard the boat that day. He was tuned into God's frequency and could hear His voice clearly when he needed it the most. Remaining grateful and seeking God in the midst of our raging seas changes the course of our lives. We no longer have to be afraid of the storms because this is where we learn to 'sail our ship.' In Psalms 107:29 it says, "He hushed the storm to a gentle whisper, so that the waves of the sea were still."

You see, God doesn't want us to pull Him into our storms; He desires to draw us into His peace. It's all about adopting His perspective in our lives. When Jesus gave orders to go over to the other side (Matthew 8:18), He was not concerned about the weather being an obstacle to His mission. Even with a storm brewing, He decided to launch out to sea.

The Lord never promised we wouldn't have storms in life. As a matter of fact, He told us to expect them (John 16:33). Instead, He promises to always be with us. He will never leave His children alone in the midst of trouble, but with trust and perseverance He guarantees we will overcome.

So as you develop an attitude of gratitude, no longer will you find yourself just waiting for the storm to pass but you'll learn to dance in the rain, assured of His faithfulness in every area of your life.

WALKING BY FAITH NOT EMOTIONS

Our dear friend and minister, Andrew Wommack, was very instrumental in my walk with the Lord since childhood. Early on he taught me how to walk by faith and not emotions. Through the scriptures I learned that God created emotions for our enjoyment; they're one of the greatest gifts we have in common with Him. What would life be without love, joy, peace, excitement or any positive emotion? They connect us with Him. It would be an empty existence without the anticipation of a baby being born, the joy of Christmas morning or rooting your favorite team on to victory. Emotions constitute one of the spices of life that make it worth living. They make the recipe complete.

Nevertheless, people often find their emotions can spin out of control. Instead of controlling their emotions, their emotions are controlling them. When something difficult or unexpected happens and they experience a negative emotion, they see it as a natural response rather than a choice. They see emotions as something they have no authority or control over; therefore they take no responsibility for them.

When I learned I didn't have to just cope or roll with the punches, but could control and have victory over negative emotions, it took me from

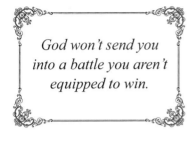

God won't send you into a battle you aren't equipped to win.

a place of surviving to thriving in my daily life. By no means have I been exempt from negative feelings, but they don't define me or my attitude. Through God's promises and lots of practice, I'm learning how to produce positive emotions in negative circumstances. It changes the outcome. I want to stress this again because I learned to do this and you can too, it is not impossible: You can learn how to produce positive emotions within negative circumstances. Emotions are determined by thought. When we start thinking in line with God's Word, He will show a way to turn any negative thing in your life around so that it works together for your good.

Though it's a blessing and exhilarating to experience the emotional highs of life, I also understand that God never intended them to sustain us 24 hours a day seven days a week. The Bible says we are to walk by faith and not by sight or appearance – that is, not by emotion (2 Corinthians 5:7).

The Lord tells us to not let our hearts be troubled. And when we come to Him with gratitude and thankfulness in any situation, the peace of God that transcends all human understanding will guard our hearts and minds (John 14:1, Phil 4:7). This is a wonderful space to remain in no matter what's going on around us. Jesus provided a way for all of us to live in emotional happiness and stability. Developing a thankful heart puts you on the fast track to improving your inner world and changing your outward circumstances.

PULLING TOGETHER INSTEAD OF FALLING APART

About 15 years ago, while preparing for my move to Colorado, I resigned from my job and was staying with my parents. Shortly afterwards, my sister's family was in transition and needed to move in with us. We had nine of us living under one little roof like a bunch of sardines packed in a small tin can. Almost overnight, I went from an independent, successful business woman with my own quaint, posh pad to unemployed and sharing two bathrooms with four adults and five children. Oh my!

Talk about an opportunity to turn madness into gladness. But honestly, this situation turned out differently than it would have for most. Yes, our love and loyalty run deep, but we made the decision, from day one, to choose positivity and peace over chaos and frustration. Every meal was like a banquet and every day was a party; sometimes more like a circus! By no means did this disqualify us from going through some tough situations; we certainly had our fair share. Yet, we learned to search for the bright side of things and chose to pull together instead of fall apart.

We cried some, laughed more and grew a lot. Friday nights became our Dinner in the Dark tradition. The kitchen would be a mess after preparing our favorite gourmet foods consisting of macaroni and cheese, peanut butter and jelly sandwiches or mini pizzas and corny dogs. After moving the furniture, we'd cover the living room floor with blankets, place settings and then light up lots of candles with classical music playing in the background. We'd even breakout our finest china: paper plates and red plastic Solo cups. It was splendid! All sitting on the floor cross-legged,

Dad would bless the meal and there'd be a smile on every precious face. I wouldn't trade those memories for the most elaborate restaurant in the world; it was fine dining southern style.

The power of praise and thanksgiving cannot be underestimated. That combination is the key to unlocking a powerful life. Many times they will be the deciding factor for success or failure in any given situation. If we'd determine to get a hold of this single principle by applying it to our lives, this world would be a much different place.

Praise and thanksgiving are key to unlocking a powerful life.

LOOK FOR HIM

For almost 20 years now, I've kept what I call *My God Kisses* journal. Every morning I recollect and write down all the wonderful things the Lord did the day before. It may be as miraculous as a healing in my body or as small as a butterfly in the backyard. But having this daily discipline has changed me because I may never audibly hear His voice but I can see His hand EVERYWHERE! It's like an internal radar system. I turn the power switch on first thing every morning and it runs on full throttle all day long.

Always believe that today is your day. God is constantly doing something behind the scenes and it's always good. Making the choice to start your morning with thanksgiving will empower you to deal with difficult things that come your way. The key word here is choice. Many times I have to choose an attitude of gratitude despite my emotions or how I feel physically. I choose to see problems as opportunities with solutions around the corner. I choose to walk in love, kindness and patience when the ones around me choose to freak out, feed negative emotions or engage in discouraging situations. I choose the provision of God's promises over the product of my bad choices or circumstances. I choose not to participate in discussions of why something can't be done because I know the outcome of that way of thinking usually stimulates negativity.

We are all going to experience setbacks and frustrations in life but the key is to never play the blame game or point our finger at someone or something else. Overcomers don't do this. Powerful people are accountable for their results and accept full responsibility for their outcomes.

As long as we focus solely on our problems rather than solutions, we can't resolve them . . . we become victims. By no means is this meant to discourage you but to empower you for better outcomes. Once you accept responsibility, you can change the results. Many times we can't control the circumstances we are in but we can control our response. However, changing the result may be as simple as changing your response. Imagine how different your family, church, business or even the world could be if everyone took personal responsibility for their outcomes.

BE A THERMOSTAT, NOT A THERMOMETER

A lifestyle of gratitude has to become your new normal; it's how God intended us to think and live. Once you stand in that space, you'll find that your worst day is equivalent to most people's good day. Your attitude will be the light that makes their day a little brighter. As a thermostat, not a thermometer, you'll set the temperature, not reflect it. You'll rise above the current mood and set a new standard just because you walked into the room!

A thankful, positive attitude is one of the most infectious traits you can possess. As they say, like attracts like. You attract who you are. Having a grateful heart is like a magnet that draws you to the right people, in the right places, at just the right time. If negative people and situations keep coming your way, it may be time to take a good look inside and examine what you're exuding. Focus on becoming what you want to attract. A cute reminder is to think of the tea kettle who, although up to its neck in hot water, continued to sing!

> *Changing your result may be as simple as changing your response.*

THE SHOE SALESMAN

Many years ago the United States was opening up some particular remote areas of the country and taking industry into those places.

Businesses were flying into these remote parts and finding ways to bring new markets in and sell goods to people. One day a plane landed on a particular island and there were two shoe salesmen aboard. After landing, they stepped off of the plane and began scouting out the land. They looked around and shortly after, one of them called back home and said, "Listen, wire me the money to come back home now, we can't do business here, nobody wears shoes!" The other shoe salesman called home and exclaimed, "Send me everything you've got, find some more money and locate more investors ASAP; nobody here wears shoes yet!"

The difference was attitude. We turn things like this into a cliché but it is absolutely the truth. There can be two people in the exact same situation but their attitudes will create entirely different results. A person with a good attitude can look at a negative situation and find a way to have success within it. However, a person with a bad attitude can look at a good situation and find everything wrong with it. And I must say, it's not a gift of the Holy Spirit or discernment when you can find out what is wrong with everything. Criticism is not a gift of God. A gift of the Holy Spirit is when you realize things are not perfect but you can still find God in the middle of it. Practice looking for the bright side. As Zig Ziglar would say, "An optimist is someone who goes after Moby Dick in a rowboat with a bucket of tartar sauce."

Remember, God didn't say there wouldn't be hard times or maddening moments, He actually guarantees there will be. However, He promises the answer is always available before the problem occurs. He won't give you a dream or send you into a battle you aren't equipped to win.

Make each day a masterpiece. Design your own method for developing a huge heart of gratitude and foster it daily, even in the little things. Then watch its rippling effect on everyone and everything around you . . . you'll wonder how you lived any other way!

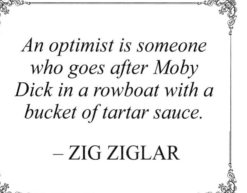

An optimist is someone who goes after Moby Dick in a rowboat with a bucket of tartar sauce.

– ZIG ZIGLAR

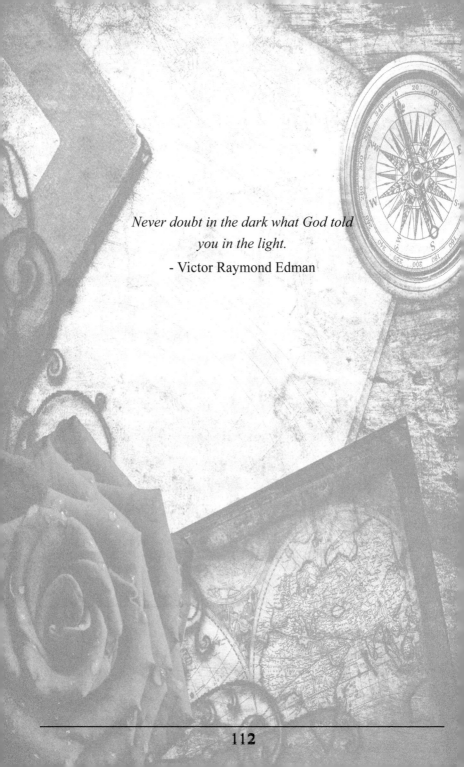

Never doubt in the dark what God told you in the light.

- Victor Raymond Edman

Key 6

Word Power

Word Power

At a young age, I was fortunately made aware of the power and significance of my words. I vividly remember a Bible teacher talking about the scientific evidence of how words actually contained matter and substance. He shared how once words are released in the atmosphere or spoken into someone's heart, they had a creative power that couldn't be retrieved or taken back. Even as a youngster, somehow I knew it was true. As years passed, I recall my peers starting to curse and say hurtful demeaning things to others. Though I was far from walking a perfect line, it would pierce my heart to hear such cutting words, yet it seemed so trivial to them.

We've all heard the old rhyme, "Sticks and stones may break my bones but words will never hurt me," and though this phrase was intended to persuade a child to ignore name calling and refrain from physical retaliation (which is good); it couldn't be further from the truth. Some of my fondest memories and most painful moments were all because of what someone significant said to me that I took to heart. Their words dug deep into the soil of my soul; some more nourishing than others.

Words are the currency of life. Even the scriptures show they create and destroy, build and burn down, save and condemn. Words have the power to heal and the power to abolish. They can be stronger than weapons in a drawn-out battle because like the human spirit, they are eternal. I've always held this visual picture of words in my mind as wanting to grab hold of something but it going right through my hands like it is invisible or transparent. They're so real but you can't take them back once you've let them go.

Throughout history, words have had as much power as the sword. Revolutions have been ignited, men have been stirred into battle and dictators have manipulated entire countries devising horrendous reasons for the destruction of countless lives; all by the power of words.

IF A MILLION PEOPLE SAY THE WRONG THING, IT'S STILL THE WRONG THING

Now, I've definitely not mastered the art of controlling my tongue or always having the perfect words of wisdom in every situation. Just ask my family. However, I've made great strides at speaking intentionally instead of reacting unconsciously. I'm realizing, more every day, that my words possess immeasurable power to shape my life and the ones around me, as well as history. I've also learned . . . if a million people say the wrong thing; it is still the wrong thing.

The Gospel is supposed to be a mirror for our daily lives.

You see, we are spiritual beings having a human experience. And as a spiritual being created in the image of God (Genesis 1:26), your spiritual genes contain the creative power to frame your personal world. This is done with two of the most powerful tools you have been given in this life; by the thoughts you think and the words you speak. The Word says, "By faith we understand that the worlds were framed by the word of God, so that the things which are seen were not made of things which are visible." (Hebrews 11:3) And it states, "You will also declare a thing, and it will be established for you; so light will shine on your ways." (Job 22:28)

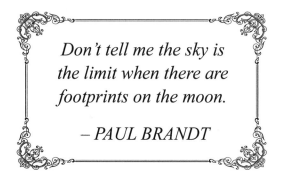

> *Don't tell me the sky is the limit when there are footprints on the moon.*
>
> *– PAUL BRANDT*

So today I want you to be encouraged. I want you grounded in the fact that within you is the very ability to ignite change, to move yourselves into action and to improve the quality of your life. The Gospel was not just written so we could be impressed with Jesus; it is supposed to be a mirror for our daily lives.

THE UNEXPLAINABLE

In 1980, my sister Tammy was riding her horse bareback, by herself, down the road from our home. Dad was not far behind when something spooked her horse and he jumped sideways throwing her down to the gravel. He was a big horse so being only 10 years old, it was a long, hard fall that left her screaming in pain.

My parents rushed her to the doctor's office but when he reviewed the X-rays, he said he couldn't touch it because the break was in the growth plate. He recommended them to a specialist nearby who completed more X-rays confirming the bad break. They tried to immobilize it with a cast but it didn't work.

They had to go back to the doctor four or five times within the next couple days as the pain kept getting worse even after trying different ways to immobilize it. Watching my sister go through such agony was heartbreaking torture for all of us. Every attempt to position her properly was unsuccessful and because they couldn't get her stabilized the pain became even more excruciating.

On the last emergency visit they put her in an airplane brace which wrapped around her body; this was the last resort before taking much more drastic steps. If this didn't work the doctor explained they were going to have to immediately admit her into the hospital to put her body into complete traction for at least six weeks. He said if it wasn't taken care of properly she could lose up to 90% usage of her entire arm and it would wither up from atrophy leaving it deformed. Sending my parents off with heavy hearts and my sister in a pool of tears, they knew this wasn't God's will for Tammy. But despair was pounding on their door. They fixed up a special bed in the living room because she had to sleep sitting up with that brace. The brace did not help; the rotation in it wouldn't keep her arm set. It was getting more hopeless by the moment.

My parents had been in constant prayer from the start but felt they needed support. Some of their best friends, Jeff and Sherry, came over to pray and they all began speaking the Word over Tammy's body. When they finished, Mom asked Tammy if she would remove the brace to see what happened without it. Initially, the thought terrified my sister; she was afraid to even move it in the slightest. With much hesitancy and fear she agreed. After they took it off, the pain completely left. Truthfully, they were all surprised it happened so fast. Dad even suggested she put it back on before going to school concerned if everything was really okay.

Grab onto Truth and speak it forth.

Because of the instant improvement, mobility and zero pain, they didn't feel they needed to take her back to the specialist. However, the doctor called to check in and when they gave him the report, red flags started flying from his end. This didn't compute in his logical mind or go over well at all; it was far beyond normal follow-up protocol. Without any notice, he turned my parents into Child Protective Services. They frightened Tammy by showing up at her school unannounced, pulled her out of class and asked her a series of questions while making her do certain exercises.

Contacting my dad after the fact was quite alarming for my parents as well, but Dad handled it gracefully. He shared the love of Jesus to that social worker through Tammy's miracle and she was deeply touched. The report they filed after examining my sister was that there was nothing they could do to improve her situation because she had full mobility. My parents decided to take Tammy back to the family doctor for X-rays and he was astonished. Her arm was still badly broken and he said there was no possible way she should have any movement in her condition. Then the Lord spoke to my mom's heart and said, "You're looking at an X-ray and an X-ray is a negative!"

In less than two weeks from the accident, Tammy was the biggest contender in a jump-rope-athon for the Heart Association and that same weekend was the high-point scorer on her basketball team at the YMCA. She's never had an issue since the moment of her miracle.

God is faithful to His Word. They say a man with an experience is never at the mercy of a man with an argument.

Our family encountered the healing touch of Jesus that night and it will never be forgotten and cannot be denied. God's love for my sister was not a theory but a tangible reality she's held onto the rest of her life. When we grab a hold of truth and speak it forth in our lives, our bodies and our circumstances, we bring heaven to earth. We usher in the unexplainable.

We've learned through the years that one of the largest obstacles to healing is not the lack of faith but the presence of doubts. When we learn to recognize that God has the answer to every situation we face and is larger than the problem that is in front of us, then the obstacles become less of an issue. The goal is to get so consumed with the answer that no roadblock or obstacle would be able to stand in the way. Releasing abundance and life through the power of the spoken Word, which lives inside of us, is how we were designed to exist. It's called faith and you can't imagine what simple faith does to the heart of God. The Gospel is Good News not good history because when it is spoken, it happens.

CHANGE YOUR THOUGHTS, CHANGE YOUR LIFE

The Bible declares that, "Life and death are in the power of the tongue, and those who love it will eat its fruit. For out of the abundance of the heart the mouth speaks." (Proverbs 18:21, Matthew 12:34) Once again, everything in the universe, and everything in YOUR universe, begins and revolves around two things: words and thoughts. No wonder they say, 'Change your thoughts, change your life.' As we take ownership of the God-given authority relinquished to us, we will move mountains. We will talk to the mountain about God, not to God about the mountain.

Examine your thought life and filter out anything you don't want to show up in your future. Make it a daily habit to inspect what your thoughts are chasing after and what your words are gathering to you. Then practice focusing on what you truly desire. Search out specific scriptures and promises for every area of your life and write your name in them.

Once again, you've got to make this personal because it is! Speak life into those desires. The life and death of your dreams are on the tip of your tongue. What are you releasing into your atmosphere? Find out for yourself what God's Word already has to say about

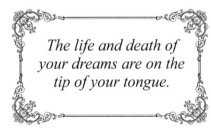

The life and death of your dreams are on the tip of your tongue.

you and your situation and fill the atmosphere with His promises on every matter. The Bible says, "For the Word of God is living and powerful, and sharper than any two-edged sword, piercing even to the division of soul and spirit, joint and marrow, and a discerner of the thoughts and intents of the heart." (Hebrews 4:12)

When we meditate on the Word of God it gives the Holy Spirit an avenue to do the extraordinary in our lives. As a brilliant teacher, personal coach and the greatest of encouragers He is able to accelerate our personal growth and success in ways unheard of to the natural mind. When He shines a light on an area of our life through the Word, if it is anything that needs correcting or refining, it's ALWAYS wrapped in love and delivered with kindness. He's able to reveal the extravagant grace of Jesus that reaches into the darkest place. His only motive is to restore what's missing in our life and reveal the greatness inside of us so it can materialize.

We've all been exposed or heard people who use the scriptures in a harsh tone to correct, judge or expose someone's weakness or sin. That can be a devastating blow to any soul and it's completely contrary to everything God represents. He never intended His Word to be abused or taken out of context.

Giving someone the truth without grace is like having surgery without anesthesia.

Giving someone the truth without grace is like having surgery without anesthesia or painkillers. Tullian Tchivdjian said, "I'm not sure there's anything worse than causing those whom God loves, to question whether God loves them." Building an unshakable loving relationship with His children is God's quest. He initiates and we respond. Being a conduit of that love should be our personal quest. God is Love. Only through the Word can we understand what Love does and how it looks. We find out where we came from, whose we are, His purpose for our lives, how we fulfill it, where we're headed and so much more!

As we are growing, there are times we need to ask ourselves what our relationship is to the Bible. Are we flirting with it, dating it, engaged to it or married to it? We need to determine if we've made an intimate commitment to it for life or if we just give it a little wink on Sunday mornings and special holidays. Just like everything else; you get what you put into it. Yet, taking a deep dive into the Word of God makes it possible for the supernatural to be routine and the unexpected to be normal. The Holy Spirit can only anoint what you know, so being a student of the Word allows God to show Himself strong on your behalf. You're taking His divine words and putting them to work in your life.

You see, God magnificently wired your thoughts to have power so you would be equipped to overcome every difficulty and rise victoriously into success. We never want to bring the Word down to our experience but we want to elevate our experience to what the Word of God says. But if we don't know where God stands on something, what He says, or how He thinks . . . it's going to be hard or next to impossible to have victory. When you meditate on His promises, then follow that up with speaking it out loud with emotion and faith, it becomes the fabric of your life. You will discover yourself in those words and it becomes part of your identity.

The power of God truly has no limits in your life and is restricted only by what you say and think. Indeed, words are free but it's how you use them that may cost you dearly.

NOTHING TO LOSE AND EVERYTHING TO GAIN

A few years ago I was working for a software company as a sales executive in Dallas, Texas. We were in the final phase of our work for a huge contract after months of legal negotiations. It was with one of the largest oil and gas companies in the country. We faxed the contract with the appropriate pricing but, by mistake, our legal department mailed out a different quote. It had incorrect pricing that was substantially lower. This was not good. When my boss realized what happened, she went into a verbal tirade and was out of control. We all knew this probably meant losing our biggest client. Not only did we have egg on our face but our integrity and reputation were at stake with the outcome very questionable.

I was sick to my stomach and nausea was kicking in. My trained mind went into solution mode.

Believe you can and you're halfway there.

– THEODORE ROOSEVELT

All I could imagine was my upper body getting stuck in the mailbox while trying to dig the letter out with a flashlight. Then after some research, I realized that would have been highly illegal. Next, I pictured myself camping out overnight at the mailbox with my sleeping bag and some hot chocolate. I'd wait as long as needed for the postman to show up, then beg him to retrieve the proposal, but that was probably illegal too. Abruptly, my boss's yelling brought me back to reality and her words were cutting deep. I could tell she expected me to give a rebuttal, but I was frozen and at a loss for words. I dismissed myself, trying to recount and review all that took place earlier. I softly shut and locked my office door behind me.

Immediately, the Holy Spirit inclined me to take action and verbally negate every single word she just spoke over this situation. It was time to proclaim God's promises over this specific contract and my life. I looked at my locked door and hit my knees in prayer. I began declaring, out loud, that the enemy had to get his dirty hands off my stuff and I claimed the successful outcome that would proceed from that moment forward. Of course, I was hoping no one could hear me, but at this point I didn't care. We had nothing to lose and everything to gain. I continued praying out loud that there wouldn't be any legal ramifications and this client would remain a loyal customer. I prayed they would agree to our proposal and this would be a winning deal for everyone. The more I proclaimed, the more real it got and the peace of God blanketed my soul. I knew from that moment forward, everything was going to be okay. No longer was it about the size of my faith but the size of my God!

MY WORDS CHANGED MY HISTORY

Well guess what? That wrong contract never made it into their hands. No one knows what happened to it; maybe the dog ate it! My words changed my history and affected everyone in that circle. My colleagues didn't know the Lord, but sure got an earful of His goodness and grace. They couldn't deny His favor upon my life because they knew I wasn't the smartest cookie in the jar; especially when it came to mail fraud. My reputation as the girl with a bluebird on her shoulder endured my entire tenure with that company but I believe eternal seeds were planted in all their hearts. It's been said, "The world does not read its Bible but it does read its Christians."

Also, the following Christmas I was humbled and blessed to be a blessing. There were eight children from a couple of poverty stricken families that were showered with gifts and love because we closed that deal. I was also able to help pay off the remainder of my parents' home and save money to pursue the dreams in my heart. This may be a small example of this principle, but I'll never be the same. I've encountered the supernatural power of God's Word.

Friedrich Nietzsche said, "All I need is a sheet of paper and something to write with and I can turn the world upside down." Take ownership of your thoughts and words to create the life you were destined to live. It's time to turn this world upside down or better yet, sunny side up!

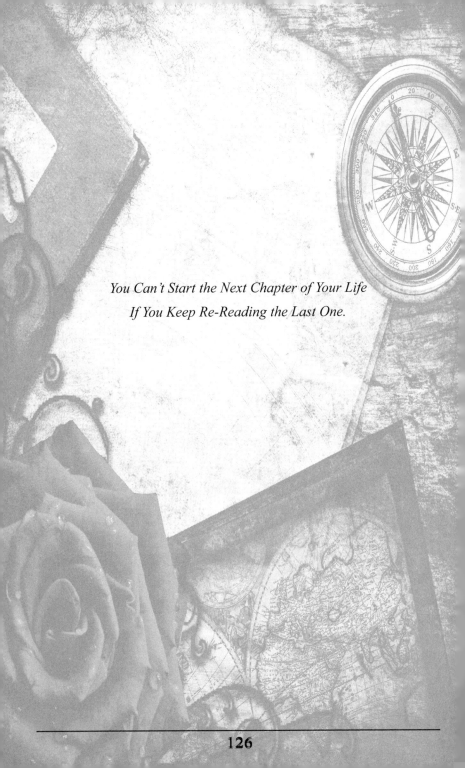

You Can't Start the Next Chapter of Your Life
If You Keep Re-Reading the Last One.

Key 7

Let It Go

Let It Go

There is a law called entropy that says anything left to itself will tend toward disorganization. This same law that works in our physical lives also works in our hearts. Therefore, if we aren't investing in an area of our life, it is inevitably falling apart. I think most of us believe this to an extent and want to improve the quality of our lives. The fact you're reading this book shows you have a hunger to grow and a desire to be all that you can be, to make your life and our world just a little better for you being in it. You must decide that you aren't willing to settle and want to squeeze out all this life has to offer.

Letting go of your past is crucial to building a quality and fulfilling life; don't let old baggage have any place in your future. Without question, there've been more destinies shattered and purposes derailed from not observing this one key: **Let – It – Go.**

I've witnessed so many people tied down by the chains of their past and then repeating them simply because . . . they won't let go. Maybe this key is for you, right now. Today, you need to know that your past does not have to determine your future. It doesn't matter where you have come from but where you're headed from this day forward. This is what you need to embrace because Jesus took everything that was wrong about you so that you could have everything that is right about Him.

One of the biggest lies Satan will try to feed us is that we can't have a quality future or a lead a life of significance because of the bad decisions we've made in the past. Do not buy into it; he is a big fat LIAR! Of course, it's essential we strive to make good choices every day, but there is always hope despite our blunders; big or small. God is greater than any mistake we have ever, or will ever, make. He simply desires that we do things His way so we can avoid hardship or suffering along the way. Like any good father who wants to protect his children, He imparts wisdom, guidance and instruction hoping we'll choose them at every turn. Pastor John Arnott says, "Sometimes we believe more in the devil's ability to deceive us, than in God's ability to reveal Himself to us."

CRAZY LOVE

The greatest constant in my life has been the ongoing revelation of God's character and affection towards me. It's not about what we do right or wrong, but how right He loves us, even when we do wrong. Even when we think we've completely derailed our destiny; He still comes after us. I call this crazy love.

It can be humiliating when we get caught doing something we know is wrong. Whether it's a child with their hand in the cookie jar or an adult hearing the sirens after driving over the speed limit . . . we all know that sinking feeling in our stomach when we've been caught. In John Chapter 8, a woman has been caught and exposed in the most shameful situation – the very act of adultery.

The story opens with the scribes and Pharisees aiming to entrap Jesus while he was in the court of the temple teaching the people. With evil motives to trick him, they threw a married (or betrothed) woman in front of him whom they had seized in the act of adultery. The law commanded them to stone a woman for this act and they said to Jesus, "So what do you say?"

A question that is rarely asked when reading this story is, "Who is this woman?" The answer may surprise you. She is you. And she is us. We have all been 'caught' in our sins. Just like when James said that if you break one commandment, you've broken them all. (James 2:10) This places all of us on the same moral level because we have all sinned.

By kneeling down and writing something shocking in the dirt, Jesus revealed the leaders' dark side and demonstrated that the law wasn't wrong. Then he said, "He who is without sin among you, let him throw a stone at her first." He wanted us to know that we are all guilty and fall short and are in need of a Savior. He wanted us to know that His love covers our exposed sin, that we are understood rather than condemned and saved rather than waiting to be stoned.

> *Jesus took everything wrong about you so that you could have everything that is right about Him.*

To the adulteress Jesus said, "Go, and sin no more." As if to say, I went down to your level, now I welcome you up to mine. I will die your death and become your adultery. I will introduce you without shame to my Father and everything that belongs to me, will now belong to you. Jesus believed that she could live that life, not because of her devout efforts or intentions of purity, but because of Him, her new friend and brother.

Don't take me wrong, sin is awful. Whether it's in the form of adultery, abusive words in a fit of rage, jealousy, gossip or lying (pick your sin), God doesn't ignore it because sin harms the people He created. But that is exactly why He sent His son to talk with us. Jesus is not a religious leader; He is a Savior. Now you can enjoy His extravagant love even after you fall into your entangling sin.

His grace ushers in forgiveness, but it also empowers us to walk in a new way. Being righteous is built on the experience of grace, not on the fear of the law or being punished. He's in the business of rescuing and releasing us, while at the same time calling our sin for what it is; self-centeredness.

Don't let the circumstances of the past dim the brilliance of your future.

Since God placed you in Jesus, you are completely perfect, holy and blameless in His sight. Jesus has replaced your old life and called you to a brand new one. Just like the woman caught in the act of adultery, your life is no longer flawed by sin, but baptized by grace. So now He says to us, "Go and sin no more. I've written a new identity and extraordinary future for you in the dust and dirt of this life."

A LIFE OF NO REGRETS

Sure, everyone has regrets. But there's a big difference in having regrets and living a life of no regrets. We all wish we could have multiple do-overs; the list is far and wide. I wish someone would've drilled into my head that, 'the longest distance between two points is the shortcut,' years before I decided to believe it. Yet, choosing to reflect rather than regret keeps me from being trapped and moves me forward. I like to say, "There's no shame in mistake-making because mistakes are simply solutions in the making." Making mistakes (even the same ones over and over again) doesn't make you weak, stupid or naive. It makes you human.

Our past mistakes never disqualify us to fulfill our God-given purposes, but can be a great guide so we won't repeat those errors in the future. Too many people are tormented with the 'if only' syndrome. If only I had finished my education, if only I hadn't married that person, if only I had chosen a different career or moved to another city. If only I hadn't started doing drugs. If only I had not taken that first drink or gone to that party. If only I had not gotten into debt. If only I had not lost my temper. If only I had followed God when I was younger. The list goes on and on.

This kind of thinking will get you nowhere fast. You must develop the habit of living out of your imagination and not out of your memory because whatever you focus on grows. You get to choose. Do you want choking weeds or stunning flowers growing in your life's garden? Start blooming where you're planted despite your current situation. Place your energy and thoughts on the future because you're going to spend the rest of your life there. The people you'll meet while pressing forward in the direction of your dreams aren't going to care about your past; they want to be in your present and some will remain in your blessed future.

The Apostle Paul said it so well, "Brethren, I do not count myself to have apprehended; but one thing I do, forgetting those things which are behind and reaching forward to those things which are ahead, I press toward the goal for the prize of the upward call of God in Christ Jesus." (Philippians 3:13) This is key!

Maybe you've been the victim of someone else's bad choices and it's plagued you for years. Sometimes those hurdles can be even more difficult to get over, I know they're real. They can do some heavy damage to our self-worth and our ability to have confidence in a brighter tomorrow. But don't let them be roadblocks to your promise land. Choose joy now with full confidence that no circumstance in your past can dim the brilliance of your future. You are stronger than your excuses and your history combined.

A PURPOSE POWERED BY HIS PAST

An extraordinary example of a person choosing to fulfill their destiny despite their past and horrific circumstances was Nelson Mandela. Born in Mvezo, South Africa, in 1918, he became a civil rights leader and fought against apartheid, a system where non-white citizens were segregated from whites and did not have equal rights. Following a protest, he was classified as a terrorist by the South African government and sent to prison for 27 years.

He spent the first 18 of his 27 years in jail at the brutal Robben Island Prison, a former leper colony off the coast of Cape Town, where he was confined to a small cell without a bed or plumbing and was forced to do hard labor in a lime quarry. As a black political prisoner, he received scantier rations and fewer privileges than other inmates. He was only allowed to see his wife, Winnie Madikizela-Mandela, the mother of his two young daughters, once every six months. Mandela and his fellow prisoners were routinely subjected to inhumane punishments for the slightest of offenses. Among other atrocities, there were reports of guards burying inmates in the ground up to their necks and urinating on them.

Finally, he was released in 1990 and continued his campaign to end apartheid. His hard work and life-long efforts paid off when all races were allowed to vote in the 1994 election. Nelson Mandela won the election to become the President of South Africa. Long after retiring from politics in 1999, he remained a devoted champion for peace and social justice in his own nation and around the world until his death in 2013 at the age of 95.

Mandela said, "As I walked out the door toward my freedom, I knew that if I did not leave all the anger, hatred and bitterness behind that I would still be in prison." Had this one man chosen to be a victim of his circumstance, the situation and history of South Africa would look very different today. If that's not turning rotten lemons into sweet lemonade, I don't know what is!

May your choices reflect your hopes, not your fears.

– NELSON MANDELA

When God says we're more than conquerors and overcomers in this life, He wasn't trying to make us feel good. He's passionate about us discovering our inheritance as princes and princesses from royal priesthoods because He wants us experiencing those royal benefits now. The Word says He's called us out of darkness and into His marvelous light so we can be victorious and overcome the world. (Romans 8:37, 1 Peter 2:9, I John 5:4) We were designed and fashioned for BIGNESS, not smallness. Our mindset should always be, 'It's not over until I win.' But you can't be victorious with a victim mentality. Nelson Mandela put it well when he said, "May your choices reflect your hopes, not your fears."

HE'S ALWAYS ON YOUR SIDE

We're all aware life has the tendency to throw some awful curve balls. There are two things to know that will help you get through difficult times. First, it's vital to understand that God NEVER engineers bad things in our lives so He can teach us a lesson or produce something good. This is completely contrary to His nature and His covenant with us. The Word says, "The thief does not come except to steal, and to kill, and to destroy. I have come that they may have life, and that they may have it more abundantly." (John 10:10) God is Love and incapable of anything outside of complete goodness. He used sickness in the Old Testament to deal with sin, but in the New Testament, Jesus bore our curse for us; forgiveness and sin were completely paid for by His atonement. (Galatians 3:13) Simply realize that the Lord wouldn't put sickness on you, take a loved one's life or threaten you any more than He would make you commit sin; that's absurd thinking. It would be hard trusting a God like that.

Knowing that God is not the author of ANY of my problems has been one of the most important revelations of my entire life. When trouble arises I know it's either from the result of a fallen planet, my own choices or from the devil. My heavenly Father has never done me or you any harm and never will. You need to know this with all your heart. It's reassuring to understand He only has good things in store for us.

Secondly, when something bewildering or difficult happens in life and you're seeking answers, don't fall prey to that pesky and weak why question. Why me? Why now? Why this? WHY!?!

This question leaves us stuck in our grief and despair and keeps us from moving forward. Courage is stripped away and our peace is diminished. The why question doesn't get answered because it's the wrong question. It usually stems from a victim mentality, if not, it will introduce you to becoming a victim very quickly.

Years ago I was dating a nice Christian guy from our church and thought life couldn't get much better. He loved the Lord and we cherished each other during those three and a half years together. We both relished the great outdoors, time with family and growing in our careers. Rarely did we argue or disagree and if we did it never lasted long enough to matter. Life was full of anticipated adventures and challenges we enjoyed taking on together.

Then one day, to my dismay, he decided to end our relationship. He'd met somebody else. My world fell apart. Needless to say, I felt hurt, devastated and empty. The rejection was so real and overwhelming that I wondered if I would ever heal or love again. I remember that evening being curled up in a ball, tears gushing from my eyes with the 'Why' question on the tip of my tongue. My heart was broken and my emotions were leading me to a dark place faster than I care to admit.

Immediately, the Lord began ministering to me and I knew I had some decisions to make in that very moment that would define the quality of my life in the days ahead. I chose to release the pain to Him. And as odd as it may sound, all the hurt left and not one more tear was shed after the first day we broke up. Jesus miraculously restored my heart back to His; back where it belonged. I had this unexplainable knowing that God was protecting me and that He didn't ask me to let go of something unless there was something much better on its way.

Everyone experiences pain, loss and disappointment in their lives and some much more than others; life doesn't always play fair. But more than seeking answers; seek God's presence and let Him comfort you. When storms hit, He longs to bring relief and blessings by working in us, around us and through us. He wants to make His love tangible. A better question might be, "What can You be for me now that I've never allowed You to be for me before?" He will always answer.

If you've struggled with this, all the more reason to let go and live. Your story needs to be told. Countless others who have gone through similar pain and battles need a voice of hope. They might only be hanging on by a thread, so to know that someone has come out on the other side could be their ultimate turning point. Why can't you be the one to help them? One day, when you hear the words, 'Because of you, I didn't give up,' or 'Thank you for sharing, I really needed to hear this today,' it will all be worth it. You'll be forever changed.

DON'T DRINK FROM THAT CUP

Another vital and necessary part to moving on is forgiveness. Forgiving ourselves and others of any wrong-doing, no matter how much it hurts is the master key to freedom from our past. God will even provide the strength to do this when it seems unbearable. It's that important to Him because He knows what unforgiveness can do to us.

There's an old story of two monks walking along a path on their way home. Nearby stood a young beautiful woman waiting to cross. The rains had made deep puddles and she couldn't step across without ruining her long, silk dress. She stood there looking very annoyed and impatient. The

Unforgiveness is like drinking the poison you intended for someone else.

younger monk noticed the woman, said nothing, and walked by. The older monk quickly picked her up and put her on his back, transported her across the water and put her down on the other side. She didn't thank the older monk; she just shoved him out of the way and departed.

As they continued on their way, the young monk was agonizing and preoccupied with what took place. After several hours, unable to hold his silence, he spoke out. "That woman back there was very selfish and rude, but you picked her up on your back and carried her. Then she didn't even thank you."

"I set the woman down hours ago," the older monk replied. "Why are you still carrying her?"

Is there anything you're still carrying that needs to be let go of? It's been said, "Unforgiveness is like drinking the poison you intended for someone else." Don't partake from that cup! It's a killer and one of Satan's favorite formulas for destroying destinies. Whether it be forgiving yourself or someone else, don't waste another second. The chains will break loose and lift a load off of your heart which you were never intended to carry. Yes, it is taking a leap of faith. It's a decision and usually not a feeling, but the consequences are eternal. And though the memories still remain and you may still feel the hurt, they'll be powerless and you'll be forever free from their hold.

UNSPEAKABLE GRACE

Often, I think about the Apostle Paul . . . if anyone could have been held back or victimized by their past, it should have been him. What a beautiful story of redemption showing that no one is beyond the saving grace of Jesus. Before he became the Apostle of Grace, Paul had a very dark side. Though a very educated lawyer and devout leader within the Jewish community and religion, his early life was marked by religious extremism, brutal violence and the relentless persecution of Christians. He was like a religious terrorist that ruthlessly lived to kill innocent Christians. He even believed he was doing it in the name of God.

Can you imagine how Paul's world must have been turned upside down and inside out when the Lord personally enlightened him to the truth on the road to Damascus? (Acts 9) Talk about some bad choices that could haunt a person's soul forever. His actions brought awful pain to many people. And yet, Paul completely surrendered his past and his life to Christ. He was not only responsible for writing over two-thirds of the New Testament, but he spread the Gospel all throughout the Roman world, doing more to advance the kingdom than most.

And this remarkable story repeats itself each day in our own lives. We are transformed by God's saving grace no matter what despicable choices we've made in the past. God did not call us to fix an old life, but to find a new life in Him; we don't go forward by looking backward.

God's a good Father and He wants to have a dialogue about the remarkable plans He has in store for you as His beloved child. He knows the antidote for your past is your future. More times than not, we don't need to be counseled about all that junk that happened to us; we need to discuss where we are heading from here. The enemy wants you to concentrate on the

> *God didn't call us to fix an old life, but to find a new life in Him.*

current facts and all the negative things that took place but the facts do not set you free. The truth sets you free!

A BETTER VERSION OF YOU

So when the past calls, let it go to voicemail . . . it has nothing new to say. Better yet, tell it to put you on the Do Not Call list. You don't have time for negative distractions. Yes, we need to learn from our past so we don't repeat poor choices, but don't judge yourself by it. You don't live there anymore and you have moved on to greener pastures and a better version of you.

One of my favorite hobbies is reading books or watching movies about people who have beaten the odds and accomplished the seemingly impossible in dire circumstances. Like Abraham Lincoln, Anne Frank, Walt Disney, Nick Vujicic, Bethany Hamilton and many others; they're just ordinary individuals who achieved extraordinary things because they didn't let their past dictate their future. They created the outcome they desired. They didn't allow people or circumstances to get in the way of a vision held tightly in their heart.

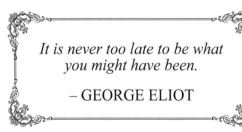

It is never too late to be what you might have been.

– GEORGE ELIOT

Everyone loves those kinds of stories and the fact is, YOU have one too. When writing the story of your life, don't let anyone else hold the pen. Regardless of your age, marital status, small mistakes or huge messes, God's grace will meet you where you are, but won't leave you there to stay. He has a way of making things beautiful again and again.

CONCLUSION

I f there's anyone who could attest to God's faithfulness, despite their humanness, it would be Abram. The Bible takes the spotlight in Genesis 12 from the history of the entire human race to one man named Abram; the first Hebrew who lived in Ur of the Chaldees. Years later, God promised him if he would leave his country and journey to a land he had never seen, God would make his descendants a great nation. Then, through them, the Savior of the world would come, all through his 'seed.' Later God changed his name to Abraham which means 'father of many nations' and he obeyed God and journeyed to the promise land of Canaan.

The Message Bible says, "By an act of faith, Abraham said yes to God's call to travel to an unknown place that would become his home. When he left he had no idea where he was going. By an act of faith he lived in the country promised him, as a stranger camping in tents. Isaac and Jacob did the same, living under the same promise. Abraham did it by keeping his eye on an unseen city with real, eternal foundations—the City designed and built by God." (Hebrews 11:8-10 - MSG)

Leaving his family and country behind, Abraham literally 'walked off his map' to follow the call of God put upon his life. They didn't have motorized vehicles, transportation or GPS systems like we do . . . talk about a humbling adventure. But Abraham plunged into the promises God had given him, finding out through obedience that God would make good on His promises. You see, we never fully understand God on a certain level until we have obeyed Him. Obedience is how we find out what God had in mind. And what a wonderful example of how perfection is not a prerequisite for God to begin His work in us. Indeed, he made some huge mistakes but what matters is that he walked WITH God and became more like Him along the way. Abraham also knew nothing he did could earn God's blessings or merit God's call on his life. They were all gifts just as they are for you and me.

Now is the time to chart your course to an extraordinary life by starting small but believing big. You were born to manifest God's greatness and glory to this world through your uniqueness and through your life. While implementing these life keys, you'll sense the invisible presence of the Lord calling you to the impossible. So, why not YOU? Why not NOW?

As you put one foot in front of the other, fear will melt away and your courage and confidence will begin to rise. Walk off your map and land onto His . . . for this is where you belong.

PRAYER OF SALVATION

Some people have said, "Well, I don't believe in God, or even know Jesus." My answer is simple, "He still believes in you, and He knows you."

His pursuit for you is real and relentless; it is with great intensity that God the Father seeks those who will be His children for now and for eternity. Come to the Father without hesitation because He sees you coming. He already has a special place in His heart that only you can fill. And God never gives up this pursuit. The Bible emphasizes: "There is no one righteous, not even one who understands; no one seeks God. All have turned away and become worthless; no one who does good, not even one (Romans 3:10-12). It says that our "Salvation does not, therefore, depend upon man's desire or effort, but on God's mercy" (Romans 9:16). Perhaps He is pursuing you now. If you are reading this, He has either sought you and bought you or He is seeking you now. You who are lost, it's time to come to the Father through Jesus Christ today; His love will leave you undone. The Bible says, "That if you confess with your mouth that Jesus is Lord and believe in your heart that God has raised Him from the dead, you will be saved." And Jesus said, "I am the way and the truth and the life. No one comes to the Father except through me." (Romans 10:9, John 14:6)

Will you come today?
Pray this prayer and start your new life today:

Heavenly Father, I come to you in prayer asking for the forgiveness of my sins. I confess with my mouth and believe with my heart that Jesus is your Son. I believe he died on the Cross at Calvary that I might be forgiven and have eternal life in the Kingdom of Heaven. Father, I believe that Jesus arose from the dead and I ask right now that He come into my life and be my personal Lord and Savior.

I repent of my sins and will worship you all the days of my life. Because your Word is Truth, I confess with my mouth that I am born again and cleansed by the blood of Jesus. I pray you will continue to reveal your love to me by your Holy Spirit. Thank you for the new creation you have made me. In Jesus' name, Amen.

Let us know that you came to Jesus on our contact page at:
www.tonyaspencespeaks.com
We will rejoice at the news with you!

ABOUT TONYA

Tonya Spence is a speaker and author dedicated to helping others find their voice, live more fully and follow their dreams. Shadowing her parent's footsteps as ministers, she graduated from Charis Bible College in Colorado Springs in 2005. Since then her hunger to infuse others with a holy passion and purpose has only grown. She believes every person is destined to reflect the beauty and glory of our King through their unique strengths and God inspired dreams.

As a Certified John Maxwell Speaker and a DISC Certified Master Trainer with Dr. Robert Rohm; she is also recognized for her expertise in relationship building and personal development. She brings proven strategies for empowering organizations and individuals to raise the bar and achieve extraordinary results, affecting every area of life.

After years as a successful professional, Tonya was introduced to the DISC Model of Human Behavior that altered the course of her life and her relationships. She provides the same principles to organizations, churches, youth and women's associations; equipping them to reach their highest potential. Tonya lives in Southlake, Texas, where she is president and founder of Tonya Spence Speaks and co-founder of The People Experts, LLC. She travels the country ministering God's Word, as well as speaking and training on personal development and communication.

She's an active member of Gateway Church in Southlake, Texas, and relishes every moment with family and friends. She also enjoys riding horses, hunting, playing softball and physical fitness while experiencing God's astonishing love in new ways every day.

Tonya Spence is available for speaking engagements through:
www.tonyaspencespeaks.com
tonya@tonyaspencespeaks.com

Notes

We were designed to get lost in our dreams while finding ourselves in Him.

– TONYA SPENCE

Notes

Sharing knowledge is powerful, but touching someone's heart is priceless.

– TONYA SPENCE

Notes

When you're facing tough challenges, it's not a matter of God showing up, but you realizing He is already there.

– TONYA SPENCE